Oh man what a life.

To my readers, I am sorry for the many mistakes in these books. As I do not have an editor, I have to try and do it all myself.

Hopefully soon Good god will send me an editor to edit these books because I miss too much and the mistakes are getting to me.

Yes my health is down more times when I am writing hence I cannot catch all the mistakes in these books and this is so sad.

It would be nice to be normal and let someone into my world, but I am forbidden to do so at this time and this is sad. It's like Moses when he had to speak to the Pharaoh and he couldn't speak, he asked God to let his brother Aaron speak on his behalf. I am in the same boat, hence I am hoping He Good God will hear me and soon. I write but I am a lousy editor.

And no I cannot get anyone to help me. When God – Good God ask you to do something for him, you have to do it by yourself no matter the mistakes you make and the hardship you incur. He must be the one to send you help not you get help for yourself. You have his trust hence you have to do right by him and for him given your limited resources.

Therefore I am hoping these books will be error free soon with his good and true help.

Know that I did not want to edit this book but my mind kept gnawing at me to do so. Trust me when your mind gnaws at you to do something you will not sleep right and each waking moment you are drawn to correct your mistakes. Hence I am doing my best to correct this book and will do the same for book two.

So hopefully I get this book revised and up on Lulu before year's end.

So if you have one of the few that has the first edition before this one; I do hope it becomes a collector's item because you have a book riddled with mistakes. ***Please note: you have to read this book in its entirety because this book is truly not what it seems from reading the first 27 pages. You will see on page 28 and onwards. And don't jump to page 28 either.***

Michelle Jean
December 05, 2014

In all I believe in and know you are my choice for a better today and tomorrow; future
You are my world
Endless love, faith, hope; dreams

In all I've found, I've found hope
Partial joy
Serenity and peace in quiet
A quiet world
Universe

It is sad that humanity truly do not know you
Care for you
Cannot truly bond with you

In all I've found, I wish I could escape it all
Find the true meaning in all of this
Find true life
Hope
You

Many sorrows are there
Many fears, but I am blessed knowing that you are with me
There for me
Protecting me
Truly loving me and not loving me so.

I see and know many things, but yet life is truly not with me; with man - humanity.
I have to say this because at times I look at the fairness of it all and find that there is no
fairness when it comes to man - humanity. No fairness when it comes to you given the state
of humanity - our sins. We are sinners, hence we sin reckless and rude and have forgotten all
about you. We are not remorseful; couldn't care less about the earth and universe; others.

In all I find, I find no fairness in the laws of men
We do to hurt and kill each other; all and this is not right.
We have no regard for life
Throw it away as if life matters not
Our soul and spirit matters not.

Many times I feel trapped, caged in a world designed for animals.
No not animals because you Good God and Allelujah did not design and create these prison
walls, man did. Man created them to cage us, control and dominate us, even eliminate us –
kill us.

Oh well this is our sorrowful world I guess.
Our hell of trusting men – so called civilized human beings.
We have to face the storms as they come.
Have to face the turmoil that man made for us.

We have to face the lies and deceit and pray that one day everything will be okay.

Yes the harvest comes and there is no escaping death's trap, hence truly good luck to man - humanity shortly.

Humanity have been judged and found guilty. Hence there is no saving grave for billions globally. The devil's day is done and there isn't a damned thing his people and society (humans collectively) globally can do about it. The devil did win over man because man did listen to him (his lies and deceit) and because of this, man was cursed by her; found guilty in all that we do.

Many still carry generational curses with them. They cannot do anything about this because the deed (curse) was done thousands of years ago; billions for some.

Man fulfilled the plan of sin and now man - humanity must die; pay.

So because of this, death comes now to take his children; his and her own.

The time is here.

The day is done and woe be unto man because the beast (death) is truly here. BABYLON WAS VICTORIOUS OVER MAN, HENCE HUMANITY MUST BOW DOWN TO DEATH WORSE THAN THEY DID BEFORE.

Babylon stands at the helm of man waving his victory flag. They (humanity) listened to the cries and lies of Babylon, hence many kill whilst billions disobey the laws and commandments of truth – life; Good God. All that we were told not to do we did. We listened to the lies of petition given by the church.

Yes the cow won. The lies of Babylon took man down and Babylon has nothing to fair because the deed was done. Man followed death to their graves. So to hell billions must go to be surrounded by the fires of hell.

It's crying time for man – humanity now. And many are going to weep. Hell has and have become a reality; hence the fears of man have and has come to pass. Hell must come down and reign on earth. In all we read about Eve and the deceit by the original Babylonians we could not listen nor could we learn. We accepted the gods of Babylon and the gods of Babylon became our gods. We threw away our gods to accept theirs and now there is hell to pay and that payment is man in the form of death, physical and spiritual death.

Michelle Jean
September 7, 2014

Many times I am confused
Thoughts are crazy
Without rhyme
Meaning
Rhythm

At times I don't know what to do
Don't even know where to begin
End

But with all this confusion and happenings in my brain, you stayed by me
With me
True to me

You sheltered me from my many storms
Turmoil's
Many sins

I don't know because today I am so not in the mood.
Mind is lost in so many different things.

The reclusive life is here again where I want to avoid everyone and everything and do my own thing.

Don't want to talk or even be around certain men - black men.

I don't know maybe it's just me.
My faults within

I am not into the swirl because there are no swirls in my book and world just men.
I am both black and white in hue; brown
I am sexual in nature
Intimate
I am everything
Hence my intimacy
Mercy

I would love to choose, but I so don't want to because I am grappling with my sexuality. And no I so don't need to be a cougar. Don't need any young things in my life to feel young. This is simply nasty. I am perfect and contented with my age hence I don't need a boy toy to feel young. It's my time to enjoy my life now that my children are grown.

And no, I am not a paper doll or a paper mache. I am fully grown hence I value and cherish the finer things in life including my good and true morals; values.

Yes I need something different and I know what that different is. The problem is, finding the right someone to share these differences with; intimacy.

I am lacking but at a specific point in time I am daring, willing to try anything. No not try anything because my sexuality is odd. Nothing lasts sexually in my world. All is just a fad and for that moment and that moment only. After the act is done, I don't want it anymore, desire is fulfilled; hence on to the next good thing.

Weird hence weird am I.

Is it right to think this way, wanting your man or woman a certain way and doing him her a certain way? I think so, hence maybe one day I will find that right someone that will go all the way, my way. But who knows maybe he or she is not designed yet; not from this world anyway.

Confused yet?
Yes

Well so am I and welcome to my world.

I guess this is just one of my lonely nights; days. One of those nights where you want to do something crazy but have no one to do it with.

No, I don't want drugs nor do I want alcohol.

No, forget the fruit juice and coffee. Yes tea too.

This is one of those nights where I want to be on the beach sitting and talking, watching the sunset whilst eating a mango or two.

If not the beach then someplace exotic will do where we could go for a walk in the dark.
Do the freak too.

New Caledonia comes to mind, but I am truly not sure if this is where I want to be.

Yes there is so much I can do in the dark.

I could be reckless and go skinny dipping but no, too much damned peeping Toms lurking in the dark. That snapshot. Lack of privacy, respect for the next human being. So no can't risk my sanity in this way.

I don't know, the people in this world are becoming more and more obsessed with insanity, nudity and lack of morals.

Damn what a life when you can't walk in the park in peace or even go to the local grocery store.

Damn I am glad I am not a celebrity.

Nothing to celebrate a part from my privacy.

Don't need the peeping Toms lurking about.
Don't need to grace anyone's camera lens with my big breasts and flat booty.

Don't need to be the next photo shoot.
Your field of dreams
You pervert.

Michelle Jean
September 07, 2014

Ah what a lonely and boring night.

Damn I'm boring.

Don't want to talk just want to write and do something different while I write.

Yes I want to get freaky but I so don't know how you will take it.

Want to talk about sex and love, doing it; whatever that it is.

Damn I'm bored and I so want to get perverted and draw you in the mix, but I truly don't know how you will take it so I had better leave well enough alone. No, I was going to go there with di well but this is a Jamaican perverted thing. So it's neither here nor there because I so don't want it to be. Stimulate your appetite you say. No, don't want to. the bottomless pit is there hence I know my limits and how far I can go. Also, if I get to my novels you will eventually know what the pit is.

Maybe one day I will show you my triple x rated side.

But then, I truly don't think I am triple x rated because certain things that people do is just nasty. And no I truly will not do.

Freak.

Okay I am freaky too. You got me so I'll lay off the freaky train for now.

Black woman we say the black man is fine and they don't do certain things. Bullshit. Many of them do do certain things. Things that you and I think only freaky white men do, they do. Wow, if only the hotel rooms and bed rooms could talk. Trust me Mr. Prim and Proper is a freak. The world some of them rock is not for me and you. Hence their freaky deeky shit they want some of us to do. Yes they can keep their golden showers because no man is going to piss on me and still have a dick. And no you can't have mine. You're just too damned nasty hence the nasty shit that you and her do. When did golden showers become clean?

Damn when did piss become healthy that some of you have to bathe in it and drink it? We are passing filth people hence the nasty shit some of you do for real. That's urine. Hence many in this world have no self respect because they do anything for money and that's truly sad.

Maybe I am sheltered.

Well yes I am sheltered because Good God and Allelujah shelters me from the storm and storms of some of these nasty and filthy men and I truly thank him for it. But with all that said, I do have a reckless side. No not reckless side just a naughty side.

I am boring and boring am I, hence I am bored and do get bored.

Yes I am freaky at times but my freaky is not freaky compared to the likes of others - some of you and the freaky shit that you do.

No, I am so not into the spanking, but trust me, if I could tie you up and do all that I want to you on any given day, trust me I wouldn't hesitate because I would.

Hey, tell me how come some of you like to lie in coffins, if not have them in your bedrooms or living room?

Is this some freaky kind of fetish?

Do you even drink blood too?

No, don't answer that because some of you do.
But for real, what's up with the coffin bullshit?

No, I truly can't think of it. Is this your way of going to hell?

OR

Is this your way of sleeping with the dead?

Damn how do you even have sex? Don't answer that because Dracula is dead or is he? Or does he lie in wait for some of you?

Yes my world is not the same as yours because I am in my own little domain that only I have the key for and to. Well Good God has it too but that's different. He's suppose to have the key and keys to our world and worlds - works.

Michelle Jean
September 07, 2014

It's September 13, 2014 and my thoughts are so different today.
It's bleak and thin. Not because outside is bleak but because of a dream that I had that caused me pain and tears, caused me to be depressed - cry.

Dreamt the beautiful flowers I gave to Good God, he made them wither and die. I could not believe he made the flowers I gave him wither and die. Hence I got upset at him when I woke up and when I thought of it on the toilet I cried. Said to myself that Good God is not capable of truth; true love; capable of truly loving me.

I gave him truth, my true love and he made it wither and die and that truly hurt me. It's like how can you give your true love; all of you that is good and true and he made it wither and die?

It's as if he does not care, he's not capable of true love like me. So I have to wonder if I am the insane one in this relationship.

Am I the only one on earth; within the spiritual realm and universe as well as his abode that is capable of true and pure love? Pure and true love that does not fade, wither or die.

I don't understand nor can I comprehend this, this scope of letting my blue and white flowers wither and die.

I am confused people. I gave Good God and Allelujah true, total truth of me without doubt and he as the Supreme Being, Father and Mother cannot handle it. So what say him to others that will now hold him in high esteem and love him true like me?

What does he tell them when they say like me; let's build a universe based on truth and true love together?

People I truly don't know because this is beyond me. It is confusing to me and does get to me.

Yes I am hurt and when I told God - Good God of my hurt and pain my chest began to hurt me.

He Good God and Allelujah cannot truly love like me.

Yes confused am I hence nothing makes sense right now. Maybe I am the one that don't want it to make sense or maybe this is his way of saying, Michelle the flowers you gave me are dying because they were not planted in the ground. They were store bought and do not have stems - roots to survive in water only. Maybe this is his way of saying we have issues that need to be resolved – worked out.

Maybe this is his way of saying he did not like them (the flowers). They weren't good enough for him. Hence doubt sets in when it comes to me and him in regards to true and good positive loving. But it's weird because I never thought of the flowers as being this way, without roots because I gave them to Good God out of joy and true love. In some way, I was hoping that he would not let the flowers wither, but let them truly grow and glow in reality.

He is my root and roots. So with him and in my eyes nothing can fade because I made him the root - true root and roots of my life. He's my rock and everything; hence all I give to him should truly live and not fade; wither and die. Everything must grow up in truth and true love. Come on now. But then this is my reality. Nothing that he Good God gives ever last. His giving is spiritual hence truly good luck in life and to life in the physical realm.

See what I do for him (Good God) and give to him (Good God) is out of pureness of truth and of my good, clean and true heart. It's like this love of truth that I have for him cannot fade because it's beautiful. So beautiful that you don't want to let go of it. This true love is my food and water when it comes to him. It's my fuel that keeps me going and I truly don't want or need this true love to fade. It's like this energy that keep you going and away from all evil.

Right now my body is changing and I am meeting people. Just this week someone tried to pick me up and a friend of mine want to get with me and I went to Good God with my issues.

People I need a relationship but I do not need a relationship based on lies, physical deceit and sexual gratification.

I do not need a relationship with someone I truly do not want or need to be with.

I also do not need a relationship with anyone for sex sake. Nor do I need a relationship with someone I cannot see myself with for the rest of my life. I am a certain way and I do not need to change this way. I need to be truly me because I am not just physical I am spiritual and the spiritual governs my life in many ways. So if you are a person that cannot comprehend the spiritual nor know not of the spiritual, then I truly don't want or need to be with you. My life is not governed by lies and deceit, it is governed by truth and the truth I have for all including Nature - Mother Earth and the Universe. I truly love her hence I see her dismay when it comes to man – humanity and their cruelty.

I am not a sexual person that lives for sex; I refuse to be. I need sex when my body needs it, not when you choose to have it. I know it's weird because your sex is not my sex. What you call sex is not what I call sex. Your sex is greed and I can't live like that. My conditioning is not your conditioning hence I refuse to have sex each and every day - daily. This is not me hence the scope of truth is not with many of us in society. As humans many of us life for self gratification and this is wrong and so not of me. My gratification is not for self, it is for all that is good and true.

Lies are not okay for me and will never be okay for me; hence I do all to move away from the lies and lying people of society. I refuse to live amongst lies hence I try and do my best to live for truth and by truth of life daily.

Yes my life is weird and boring but this is the life I chose for me. Hence certain things that he Good God do and does will hurt me. Like I said, he is my root and roots and I was not expecting him to let the flowers I gave him wither and die. I did not give them to him out of lies, I gave them to him out of truth and true love; joy.

People I was so excited when I saw the flowers in the grocery store that I bought it for him. They are blue and white - beautiful.

They (the flowers) still have life but the blue is fading. But the flowers are still gorgeous just like him. I truly don't know why he would let them fade in his world; our world of truth and true love. Now here I am confused that He not me; but He let the flowers wither and die.

Like I said, maybe he cannot truly love like me but in truth I really don't think so. He knows I am only human and no matter how I try, I can only give him good and pure; clean thoughts in the spiritual sometimes. I cannot give him anything physical not even his 25 million dollar mega mansion; at least not yet anyway. I do have certain needs and wants and when I get that I am good to go. As it is, I refuse to let anyone come into my life and take him from me. I refuse this because I like doing things with him and one of those things is going shopping with him even though I can't see him. He's not human but I have to include him in the mix. My spiritual being knows him to a large extent; it's my physical that truly have to get to know him and be with him. Yes this is hard but when you truly love then it does get easier to know him.

I'm very protective of him in this sense hence my lifestyle is not normal to some of you. I more than truly need him Good God and Allelujah and when he does certain things they do hurt. SO YES, JUST AS WE HUMANS HURT OTHERS AND OR HIM, HE GOOD GOD CAN HURT US TOO AND DO HURT US IN HIS OWN WAY.

Sad yes, but this is the reality of life I guess. Oh well, I guess I am learning all over again because I had him Good God on a pedestal, a pedestal that could not be rocked by anything and here it is, I am being rocked and hurt by him. I know I did something wrong somehow and that wrong I have to discover. Maybe that wrong has not happened yet but yet my flowers given to him he faded, made wither and die.

No people I can't lose him. So Good God whatever it is in time that will cause me to hurt you for you to leave me, truly do not let it happened because I cannot live without you. Like I've said, I truly don't want to die and if you left me I would truly die. So whatever evil that is set in time for you to leave me, I am truly asking you to move that evil out of my way.

You cannot let anyone come in and separate us. I refuse this separation hence take all evil out of my way - our way more than infinitely and indefinitely forever ever without end. Like I've told you and humanity, you are my right, so why now are you going to allow someone and or something to take my right, You from Me? This isn't fair to me and you. If the land I want to go (Luxembourg) is the cause of you letting our flowers wither and die, then I will infinitely and indefinitely never ever go there forever ever. I refuse to lose you over a land and their people. I know this is not the first time I've made mention of Luxembourg hence something is wrong somewhere with the land and people for you to cause the beauty I've given you to die. ***Now I ask you; what wrong did this land and people do to you for you to feel this way about them?***

What did they do for you to be against them so?

Yes I know now that this land is forbidden to me so I had better leave well enough alone.

So for us Luxembourg is off our radar of places to go. I truly don't want to hurt you hence I am listening but you could have told me in another way. You did not have to let the flowers I gave to you wither and die. You did not have to truly hurt me like that come on now. We are good talkers, well I talk your ears off all the time but don't do it again because you know my more that infinite and indefinite true love of you. You also know my temper too. You did not have to make me cry in this way come on now. You know my feel and how I am with you so no more hurt and pain. And I am truly sorry if I hurt you by saying I want to go to Luxembourg. Truly sorry for going on the internet and trying to look at vacation spots there.

So smile and know that I will not willingly and or knowingly hurt you. There are lands you truly do not want or need your people to go to and Luxembourg is truly one of them. But Good God with all this said, you need to let your people know which land (s) they are to avoid and or forbidden to go to. Losing you is not an option nor is it worth it. So truly talk to us and do not leave us hanging. We need to know each forbidden lands right away. Come on now.

You need to help me get your true message across.

So on this day, let us truly forgive each other and move on. We have to do this for our sanity and the sanity of others.

Man I thought I was picky but I know you are picky too. There's no denying you that's for sure because you are my protector and I am truly yours.

So where too next?

Samoa in the South Pacific is still on my radar hence if I could live there I would. Good God di people dem fat eeen. I know I've told you this before but I can't get over the people because they are gorgeous. Pleasant to look upon. You know what Good God, one day we have to do the Samoan Vacation our way. No for real because I so want to sleep outdoors and we are so going to real soon.

No not the Hawaiian thing but the Samoan Vacation, yes the Samoan Way. No pork though because you know how filthy and nasty the swine (pig and or hog) is in the spiritual realm.

Pork is forbidden meat for me and your kids - children and people. Yes beef too. Beef is true evil hence the meat of cows your people are truly not to eat period. Beef and or the cow is associated with the demons of hell - true and pure evil and this is why the Babylonians worship the cow. It is sacred to them. But with all that said, I do eat beef but not all the time. I prefer veal over beef for some strange reason. *And please note: Good God did not tell me beef was forbidden to eat. When he does, I will put this meat on the forbidden list. But pork I know is truly forbidden; a no no to eat and or consume for the children and people of Good God.*

Chicken we can eat.
Lamb we can eat.
Goat we can eat.
Fish we can eat but creepy crawlers I refuse to eat.

Certain things are forbidden to eat, but it's up to you to know what you can and cannot eat under the guidelines of truth – cleanliness.

Remember many of us do not have the same god; hence what is clean for you is unclean for me and what is clean for me is unclean for you. So know the god you serve and or gave your life over to. My god is not your god so my laws and or the commandments of God – Good God and Allelujah do not apply to Billions of you.

Know that my God cannot save billions of you because you did not choose life, you chose death hence death must take billions of you in the end shortly.

And even though many of you say Allah, I cannot save you if I am the saving grace because you mock life and go against life. You knowingly and willingly kill. Thus disobeying the "thou shalt not kill," commandment – law.

But in truth Good God, I truly do not like to see animals being killed. So if it be thy will, real soon let me consume more vegetables and less meat.

Truly wane me from eating so much meat.

Thank you.

Michelle Jean
September 13, 2014

Ah Good God because the mind is weird this month and I so do not know why. The vibe is there but my thoughts are jumbled up because death is on a different level; track.

I'm not sure about George Clooney and his family; if there is going to be a death because this dream is jumbled up and confusing, so I will truly leave it alone. I am not sure if I saw the death of his father which would mean his mother is going to die. So you know what, let me leave this alone because I am so not sure.

Dreamt about Shaq. The dream is strange too because I can't remember if we went on a shopping spree so this dream I am going to leave alone as well and or too. Too many weird things in the dream world. And I don't need my brain to be overloaded by too many things.

It's weird because I was walking alone somewhere and that somewhere was different. All White People but this is normal for me. Truly don't care if I am walking amongst all White People. They do not mind me and I truly do not mind them because we are ancestors and they are a part of my good and true family tree.

Yes not all but some. Hence Scotland is my key, one of the keys to my life and existence; ancestry.

Truly want and need to go there. Maybe one day when they are not attached with or to England and all the bullshit of England naturally.

Oh God - Good God how wonderful and blessed if all the land and lands I hold dear to my heart can come home to you naturally in truth and unity.

How wonder it would be if we could raise our glass to you and say, truly thank you for being with us and holding us true and dear to your heart, truly well done.

How wonderful it would be if we could come together in unity and raise up our country and countries including people prosperously globally financially, spiritually and health wise.

Oh Good God truth would be our course because we would be honest and true to each other. We would truly love each other and be clean in all that we do for others and each other.

Unification, unification Good God. How good and true this would be between You, Me and all our land and lands of truth.

We would be dignified with good morals.

We would truly love and be free.

We would not have to contend with the lies of sin of man anymore because we would be truthful and truly loving to each other and you.

We would be infinitely and indefinitely sin free, void of all lies and deceit.

Our land and lands would strive in goodness and truth.

We would plant naturally; organically.

We would be morally sound because we would have good morals.
Truth

We would live for life and not death.

We would share equal and good with each other.

We would not fight amongst each other.

We would be our brothers and sisters keeper in goodness and truth.

We would be good and truthful citizens.

You would be in the midst of all that we do that is good and true; right because no evil will be in our land and lands. No evil would be in the midst of us. All would be good and true

No death would there be.
No sorrow or pain would there be.

No wrong would we do because you would be our good and true keep all the time. Respect we would know to give you and will give to you because you are the God of all. Hence you are Allelujah - All and we would be truly united in all; good will. You.

Ah Good God, why can't this be our good reality here on earth and in the spiritual realm? Hence my heart weep and bleed for all that is good and true between me and you; our good and true people; family.

Michelle Jean

Ah Good God, remember Scotland in their time of need - troubles. Truly remember them and hold them firm to you.

Truly lift them up so that they can overcome the curse and evils of the devil.

Lift them up so that they can be free of the devil economically, physically and spiritually globally one day.

Good God, also remember my beautiful mother on this day because her birthday comes soon and if it be thy will let me see her so that I can tell her I truly love her and miss her.

Good God, truly do good by her for me because she is my blessing from you and I truly love her more than infinitely and indefinitely unconditionally.

I know she's with you but one day I will see her and walk hand in hand with her like lovers - true lovers do.

She is my queen and king just like you.

She is my heartbeat and soul just like you.

You are both truly loved hence truly thank you for her.

Good God truly thank you for being you and giving me her.

My heart is there for you in truth, so truly take care of my physical and spiritual heart; You and my wonderful mother.

Truly let's make the jealousy fade because it seems when you don't like something my heart begins to hurt.

This has to stop because the pain of the heart is not good and it seems I am getting these pains more and more as I write this book.

Yes, I have to get my heart checked out because this pain is annoying; as if something is toying with my heart for me to die.

I hate this feeling hence you know me and doctors; hospitals. I avoid them every chance I get. If the pain persists I am so going to go to the hospital because this feel sucks.

Ah God it sucks to be sick. Hence I have to do more to get my health in check naturally; organically, physically and spiritually.

The medicines are not working because the more I take them the sicker I get. Yes my eating habits need to change hence I so can't stand the processed everything. Need to be some place nice and warm so that I can enjoy the sun and the organic everything. Yes the health is going again because the time has changed; weather getting colder and my body so cannot take the cold. I need to be somewhere or someplace warm so that I can walk. To be honest with you Good God, I don't know how I am going to manage this winter. I so don't want to be caged inside but it seems I'm going to be this winter again because I truly cannot afford to go away for three months to a place, someplace or somewhere warm and nice and void of crime and violence; theft and heartache including hard ache.

I truly need a vacation right now because it's getting cold and depressing. Yes I want to go home but can't because my homeland is too dirty and I cannot disobey you. But yet I am stuck here and it sucks.

I cannot move anymore and this is sad.

I need to move but restrained; can't and this is so so sad.

I so want to abdicate but my life is at stake. Hence I have to settle myself and yearn like the rest of the people that want to leave but are trapped in lands that they truly do not want to be in. Lands that they do not have any rights in.

The depression starts.
Anger flows for being stuck around people you truly don't want to be around.

Damn why can't life be different for me? So different to the point where as soon as I say I am bored and want to go away, I go away right away without any strings attached.

Why couldn't I be financially stable and not so financially poor that I can and or could afford to take a trip on my own to anywhere? Well to lands that are permissible for me to go in.

Damn my life sucks because I truly want to be on my own but can't.

Damn the thoughts of the mind sucks because I truly do not need to be like others that use people nor would I. I guess I have to be this way until better comes for me. I know the better but getting there is the process and problem.

No, I will not blame single motherhood anymore. My children are grown and it's time for me to save and leave - take that perfect vacation.

Hence Samoa here I come for real literally.

Michelle Jean

I so got to go and it matters not where I go.
No it matters.

Body has changed.
Thoughts have changed
Feelings changed to a certain degree.

Yes I so got to go and it matters not where I go.
No it matters.

It matters to me hence I truly need you to journey with me.
Need you to come on a vacay with me.

We could do the beach thing
Reading in the hotel room thing
Sleeping thing

Yes we can wine and dine each other
Ah yes let me feed you
Hold your hand and tell you I truly love you

We could dance to a song or two

Yes it would just be you and me
Them
Us
The others

Ah yes the bed
Just know it won't be me and you
It will be me you and them
Many

In the morning when we awake we will have breakfast together. But before we do, I will wash your face and brush your teeth; even bathe and or shower you.

You know me and my weird feelings when it comes to bathing you.

Yes this is my right and my thing to do, so don't you dare want to change this.

Yes I truly love to feel you
Touch you
Watch you melt as I bathe you.

Ah my darling and king including queen, when are we going to vacay together?
When am I going to bathe you in the sea?
Damn I need to dress you

Lotion your skin with Japanese Cherry Blossom Lotion not just anything.

Ah the things I want and need to do with you and to you. But for now we will share a bottle of wine or two; even a beer because we are not limited to wine.

Fruit juice of the exotic kind will do.

No sugar added just naturally and organically sweet.
Flavoured

We could share a treat.

Ah yes the Jackfruit because it will be outlined on the belly for me to eat.

Yes it's meaty and juicy hence it's one of my favorite fruits if you know what I mean.

Damn I'm thinking about the armpits because I will play with your hair. So if you are a man that loves to shave the armpits stop it because I truly love my fun and play; playing with your hair. And no the mind is not limited to the armpits hence my basketballs must have hair. Hey you can't dribble bare but you must have hair.

Must have dem hairy legs too but not too hairy like a bear. Hair must be just right on all your body parts; underarm parts do you hear.

Damn boy stand for me
Let me bask in your manliness

No I don't need your feminine side just yet
Don't need you to shed a tear

When I do you will know
At times it will be automatic

Hey I'm strange this way; hence it's you and me, me and you all the way.

Michelle Jean
September 13, 2014

For me this is true love hence I truly do not want to leave you
Truly do not want this feeling and vacation to end.

Oh next time let's jet away to Paris
Iceland
Greenland

We'll take a boat to the Mediterranean
Maybe
Ah the yacht

Hey we can hop over to Russia and take a train
A train to where is the question and new story.

Hey on that boat we could find each other
Talk and make love to FOR YOU By Kenny Lattimore.
Yes I truly love the oldies better.

We could truly commit to each other in truth.
Become truly divine
True love
Pure and good everything.

We could laugh to a joke or two.
Just who the comedian is that will make us laugh is the issue.

Do I want them onboard our yacht?

Hell no! A DVD will do.

We will have dinner for two.
Make a smoothie or two.

Do I need more than a day or two on this boat; yacht?

No, because all I will do with you on the sea I will do.

We will full joy because I will take and have it all; all of you that is if you know what I mean.

Michelle Jean
September 13, 2014

Boy stand at attention for me
Let me explore you
Devour you

Oh shit you can be my Jamaican Cheese
Stone ginger wine too

Damn boy you can be my Jamaican Overproof Rum; ruff going down.
Hard
Tart
Harsh and refreshing.

No, no let's stop because the candlelight in the bathroom will do.

The wine filled glass all around.

No don't need any towels, just a rose pedal in each glass with the finest of wines.

Yeah baby, specialty made tarts for me and you to enjoy.

No, no you can't make mine breast size; they are way too big for the cup. And you know dem small size tatas are not for me. You know me and big things. The way I love big jackfruits and not them skinny things.

Don't like pipe dreams either, hence the pipe have to be the right size and yes, cut to fit me and not them or her.

You get the picture because I will wrap, tap and take.

Yes it will be great because you are my practice and everything if you know what I mean.

Dare

Michelle Jean

It's Saturday and the body and mind is talking, telling, needing.

Boy let's add a little flavour and savour.

For a change let me do what I need to do.

I need to be your bedroom bully and take everything.

Need to rock your boat
Savour your whip. So let's hope it's fully seasoned for everything; good for the ride.

No, no, I don't need any meat tenderizer
I'll do that and more

Pull tug
Draw
Aah the Rough Rider

Rough Rider
Deicer
Cleaver

Damn boy I'll be your chocolate cookie
Chocolate flavour
Yeast and natural riser

Damn the tongue because I hope you have some good tongue action. I was told I was an inexperienced kisser. So you had better be able to teach me. Teach me the right moves and grooves, tongue action, and tongue everything.

Yes the waist is rusty but for you, I'd fly to Africa and let them teach me everything when it comes to African grooves; moves.

Waist movements.

Better yet African everything.

Wow, we are so not limited, the Blue Nile
White Nile too.

Come on baby take a walk in my park.

Long and short walks are fine hence the strokes of your spokes (bicycle); ride.

Michelle Jean, September 13, 2014

Yes people the mind is going hence I have to stop things here. The days are getting cold and lonely and I am cherishing peace and quiet more and more.

Want to be in my own world where I do not see anyone but me and that special someone for that brief encounter.

Flight

Need to be amongst nature and feel nature. Not human nature but nature nature; the trees. Hence the brief encounter; all I need.

Ah man if only I had my own private island somewhere in Africa
The South Pacific
British Columbia

If only I had all the trees that I could ever need and see.
Need the rain and sunshine to warm and fill my heart all day long.

Yes the joy and pleasure of nature and not having anyone to disrupt my solitude.
Yes no peeping toms or next door neighbours.

I can scream all I want.
Enjoy what I want when I want.
Take him how, when and where I want.

No stress will I have because I would not have to worry about the hustle and bustle of society (cars, planes, trains - automobiles).

No grocery stores nearby
No shopping malls
Theatres

Just solitude that I can and will enjoy; be myself; on my own.

Ah yes the crazy thoughts come now and no they are not so lonely anymore.

Michelle Jean
September 13, 2014

Yes I dare to dream of me and you
Dare to dream of your long legs wrapped around me

Dare to dream of us making love under the stars
In the bushes
In the trees

We can do it rough
Mild
Strong
Hard

We can play
Or
Just lay naked under the stars.

No wait the prying eyes of Google
The Paparazzi
Him or her lurking in the dark – bushes
The peeping toms.

Damn there goes that thought because we are so not private. Eyes are still watching - the nosy neighbours with the long range lens; infrared.

Ah we must come with another thing.

Yes I have it and we will make it, bulletproof, infrared proof, lens proof but not star proof. I want to see the stars and be one with the stars in all I do in the nightly things with you.

Yes I dare to dream
And those dreams are of me and you.

Yes you have to be overprotective.
Truly loving and affectionate because when I give the universe glows, flows, dance in awe; glee with me and you.

Michelle Jean
September 13, 2014

Good God this has been a frustrating day. I'm so sick of these major corporations that offer superior and good service but give crappy and stinking service to no service at all.

I have Bell Internet and Home Phone. I had their satellite but got rid of it because I was paying way too much money for duplicated channels and channels I don't even want to watch; need. Besides the kids enjoy Netflix so they have this service and are extremely happy with it. They can watch the programs they want to watch when they want to watch and this is great. Netflix truly do not change your services but if you can, add CNN and some other news channels and carry some updated programs.

Have a Canadian and American News Channel and if you can add a Korean Segment of shows because their shows are nice. Have to finish watching the ones I've started. And yes have English subtitles for the Korean and or Chinese drama and comedy. Also have a Jamaican and or Caribbean Channel as well as African channel that show comedy, music, drama and news. No, I am sick of the same old same old with these companies that don't cater to your needs. They do not see the needs of their customers hence they box you into their dead end programming that no one truly wants to watch; need.

I am paying for your service, do not give me what I do not need or want. You want my money, so cater to me not me pay for your crappy service that doesn't work like the internet.

It is so bleeping frustrating how Bell offers high speed internet and you are paying for high speed internet, but yet you cannot get onto the internet. You keep getting DNS error and when you speak to a representative they're telling you the service is fine it's your computer. How the bleep can it be my computer if my computer is working fine?

I can't keep calling you and reporting this problem and nothing is truly being done about it. If you can't fix the damned problem from your end what the hell am I paying you for?

What?

My life is damned stressed out already; I do not need you to add more stress to it with your lack of services and or no service thereof.

Is the monthly internet fee that I am paying you for me to get frustrated by you and your crappy service?

Where in our agreement does it say, I will pay you for crappy and no service?

You don't credit people for your errors but yet you want us to pay our bill on time for shit.

Get your bleeping act together because no one should be stressed out over your lack of service; poor technology. And Norton don't say you have good internet security and block my internet service provider and or screw them up. I have to get you into the mix too because your internet security is not internet security. It is flawed. And this is from reading on the internet that your internet security can do this and this is wrong if this is in fact true. From experience, your security does not wipe off all my virus on my computer because I still get this message saying I have 22 errors that need to be fixed and your virus protection cannot fix the issues. Maybe I have the wrong one but who knows. Do not sell things that truly do not work. Don't scam people because you of yourself would not like to be scammed.

KNOW THIS BELL. THERE ARE PEOPLE OUT THERE THAT ARE SICKLY LIKE ME THAT NEED THE INTERNET.

Some of us need to call for a nurse to discuss health issues and if they can't get on the internet to get the phone number for the nurse what then?

And forget about emergency services at your local hospital because some of us like me don't care to go. If I can talk to a nurse that is fine. But if my internet is not working how the hell can I contact them? I could go there with my kids and homework but I will not go there because in truth they truly don't do homework. My niece does and it's frustrating when she comes to my home to use the internet for homework purposes she cannot get on because the internet does not work.

And no, I do not have a refrigerator magnet so don't go there. This (magnet) the doctors and or government should make readily available to all in Canada but unfortunately, it isn't and or nothing is being done for people to get these magnets if there are any with medical contact numbers on them.

Yes people I am so frustrated with these damned internet providers. Plus I am fed up of the programs they run in the background to make your computer go slow. Why provide a service that frustrate people royally to the point of wanting to break the damned computer.

You are stressing me out with your crap and I am sure you are not going to pay my medical bills when it comes to your crappy and unnecessary services that case me undue stress and pain; heartache.

Don't take my money if you are going to anger me.

Do I want credit from you right now or in the future?

No. All I want is for you to come and take your crap so that I can find another internet provider that's going to make me and my life truly happy without the crap I am facing with you and from you.

That's the problem with these big corporations. When you get too big you feel that people are going to stand for your crap. Well I'm not going to stand for it hence I don't want a credit from you. I just want your crap to be gone. Trust me if there was a way to sue your ass for my pain and anguish for dealing with you I would just to teach your ass a lesson. Trust me if I could I would. And yes, I would donate the entire settlement to charity because I truly don't want your dirty and corrupt money.

Don't take my money and scam me.

Don't give me customer service reps from across the continent that can't speak proper English either. I am Canadian; keep the damned jobs in Canada. I don't want or need to speak to someone in India or Mexico or wherever. I want and need a Canadian Customer Service Representative that knows about my problems and issues. Don't reroute me because the funds I am paying you isn't foreign funds, it's Canadian, Canadian Funds. Why the bleep should my money fund other countries citizens? Come on now.

We want the jobs in Canada but because of greed you out source and neglect your own. Bleep you, take your shit out of my house/apartment and don't come a knocking on my door again with your damned customer appreciation letters. Appreciate this - yes my ass. Kiss it. I refuse to represent a company that outsource their jobs to another country. I did not go into a contractual agreement with another country. I went into one with you in the country I am living in. Do not get someone else from another country involved. My personal information should not be in another country, it should be in mine; the land I reside in. This is a violation of my personal rights and every company that do this including banks should be charged for breach of trust and identification theft.

I am so sick of you corporations breaking the law and think you can get away with it. Come on now.

I trust you and you are breaking my trust by sending my personal information to another land that do not have my best interest at heart. How would you like it if someone was to send your company's personal information viral and or to another country?

You sure as hell would not like it, so why the bleep are you doing it to me and others?

I am fed up man hence I have to vent in this way.

I need the internet to print your bill because you charge me $2.00 per month for me to get my bill from you. Talk about extortion and highway robbery.

I'm to pay your stamp and paper fee. So all around I am paying for you to extort me. You are saying to me, if I want this I have to pay for it.

Ridiculous and pathetic hence soon many of you are going to lose it all globally. I am so glad that the harvest is coming where wicked and evil people including companies such as you Bell will lose it all in less than a day.

Bunch of thieves that have not good thoughts or deeds for your customers.

Good riddens to many of you. Who the hell needs ya? Hence I am going back to the old fashioned way - the mail. Who the hell needs a e-mail or g-mail when you can't connect to the internet; your mail.

Scam artists is what most of these corporations are. All they see is the bottom line whist ripping off their customers.

Fed up I am hence I loathe technology that do not work and or a heartache and pain.

There must be a better way when it comes to the internet. There just has to be.

Oh ya, snail mail - our daily mail.

Technology has become too damned complicated and stressful. There's no ease of use just heartache and stress; perverts that like to hack into your computer to look at your nudes. Bitch there's playboy and playgirl for that. Wait, are they still around?

No, come on now. You cannot live your life in private lest someone hack your computer and watch you do the nasty with your significant other and or get off on your naked selfies.

Shit, what's the use of these porn sites or companies when you can invade someone's privacy for free?

To you hackers not because you are tech savvy means you should invade someone's privacy. My privacy is private hence leave me the hell alone. Tell me something, how would you like to be hacked and your personal photos - life be broadcasted to the world?

Some of you wouldn't, so why do you think the next person would?

But then again, I refuse to defend anyone because I truly don't know why you would want to take nudes of yourself and leave them on a computer?

Computers have never been private hence the global peeping Toms (Perverts) that like to hack and tap into your privacy - private life and watch you.

Damn these technological peeping toms that do the human salute of a different kind watching you.

Michelle Jean
September 13, 2014

Yes people I just vented and I needed to do this because I am finding accessing the internet a hassle; frustrating.

Why the hell should you be paying for something that do not work?

Yes the internet is a necessity for some and in some ways it is for me because this is how I connect to Lulu. Lulu.com

I use the internet for many things including music because I end up in places where I don't even know how I got there. Hence I have to have the internet working when I need it.

There are certain things I want and need to do hence I have to explore.

I didn't even know there was a Sudanese Fashion Week. There's a Jamaica Fashion Week but Sudanese Fashion Week. Wow.

So Sudan here I come when it comes to your fashion. Need to see it so you had better bring it; bring fort your best for me to see and endorse. And to the Sudanese Government both North and South, squash the feud because the fight is over. You are one people and no one should come in and divide the two. Good God is not a religion he is life, so I suggest you find a common ground and work out your differences because religious lies gets no one into heaven and or the abode of Good God and Allelujah, it gets them into hell and fast. Life reside in Sud, Sudan which means south of Gan – the Garden of Eden, so truly know your history and where you are coming from. Life joined in Sud – Sudan and that life is the White and Blue Nile. Sudan is the junction and or the resting place of Man, so stop disrespecting Life – the life Good God gave you to keep.

Yes I am mad hence I wrote this and it is harsh. You will not like me but you cannot say you are Sudanese and disrespect all life form including your own. Yes you can hate me but no one can hate the truth of self – life. Good God did not give us religions of death to live by. HE GAVE US LIFE, HENCE LIFE IS EVIDENT IN AFRICAN LANDS AND THAT LIFE IS THE BLUE AND WHITE NILE. This source of life is great but yet no African can see this because we've forgotten where we came from. We are hated by everyone including our own but yet we say we are God's – Good God's people.

So here me now and here I go. Sudan, North and South Sudan, truly look at your beautiful people because both governments disgust me. Make my stomach sick to the point where I don't want to be black anymore. You sicken me to the core to see how you treat your own. You make me hold my head down in shame and disgrace to call myself black. You are Africans but yet you treat your people worse than dogs. You've given up all your African pride and now look at you. You make people look down on the black race. You make whites come in and show your people wallowing in filth like pigs and dogs hence it grieves me to the core. Like I've said, we were kings and queens that has been reduced to worse than swines begging the European Nations and United Nations for their slop – leftovers and for this I truly hope Good God truly and fully walk away from all of Africa; African Lands; the lots of you. *Yes I know this is wrong Good God but when I see the hypocrisy of these damned Alaskans it makes me sick to my stomach. I don't want bleeping White Hope; I need the* **BLACK RACE TO SMARTEN UP AND DO BETTER FOR SELF AND HELP EACH OTHER. I NEED AND WANT BLACK HOPE.** *These people are not there to help Blacks. If they were, their race would not design and or create diseases to wipe us off the face of the planet. Enough is bleeping enough. You don't like us stay the bleep away from us. Africans are not your damned guinea pigs. We are not lambs going to the damned slaughter house and it's time all of Africa bleeping wake up and truly save their own. We are not damned beggars that live amongst flies. I am sick and tired of the Black Race being showed and depicted like this. No, I am tired of these scunt holes using us like we are their bleeping commodity that begs them for their tainted handout of sickness. Africa bleeping wake up and go back to your African roots. Stop letting people show us as being deprived and needy. We are not a deprived race of people. We are a people that has been raped and abused by everyone including our own. We are the ones to create the heavens and earth not them. We are the ones to create these lands not them. We are the advanced and civilized ones not them. So stop letting people that have not the best interest of All Africans steal our pride and dignity. Come on now.*

Don't bleeping go into African lands waving the **WHITE FLAG BY SAYING YOU ARE THERE TO HELP WHEN YOU ARE THERE TO KILL THEM; THERE TO TAINT THE IMAGE OF AFRICANS AND SPREAD YOUR PROPOGANDA ABOUT HOW THIS DISEASE AND THAT DISEASE CAME FROM AFRICA WHEN YOU DAMNED WELL CULTIVATED THESE GERMS IN YOUR LABORATORIES AND BRING THEM TO AFRICA. YOU INFECT PEOPLE HENCE EVERYWHERE YOU GO YOU GIVE OTHERS YOUR GERMS TO KILL THEM AND TAKE THEIR LAND AND HISTORY. YOU ARE THEIVES HENCE THE MOUNTAIN OF GOD – GOOD GOD DOES NOT HAVE MANY OF YOU ON IT.**

Yes I am being racist but it burns me to the core as to how much or many black people in America that is bleeping rich but care not for Africa.

Look at the rappers, athletes, news castors, business men and women that have millions at their disposal that would rather spend their money on fake boobs, fake asses, fake hair, fake face, prostitutes, skinny and stinky pum rather than help their African brothers and sisters – yes African own.

No wonder some of you go broke because you have no good will for your African own. But yet you say you are African American this and African that.

Look at how much some of you spend on expensive cars, houses, jewelry, bling as you call it, but yet in all that you do, you do not think of your African brother or sister that need a helping hand. Good God helped some of us so help him and help your own. Africa needs you but according you, you do not need Africa. Yes this is your actions that are saying this. It blows my mind how some of you blow millions on strip clubs – lap dance but yet cannot think. All that money you blow in a strip club can buy medicine for your African own.

All that money can be invested in your future as well as Africa's future. Come on now.

All that money you blow can buy a house or two for your African own.

All that money you blow can help an African farmer start his or her own business or even build his or her dream farm; home.

All that money you blow at strip clubs and clubs can help an African nation pay down their national debt to the International Monetary Fund (IMF).

All that money that you blow can pay for thousands of African children to go to school.

All that money that you blow can help pay for school fees
Modernize a hospital or two

Provide clean drinking water and or build wells in communities that have none.

All that we say we are, we've become nothing but slaves working to build others, but yet cannot see the needs of our African own and build our own – our African home.

Look at how much money some of you spend on a lousy pair of shoes.

Look how much we spend on fake ass hair and human hair to look ridiculous and stupid globally. Everyone one profits off us hence we build other nations and leave our own in ruin. We do not invest in us. We would rather invest in others whilst neglecting our own. Look at it Good God, we spend over a billion dollars per year globally to tell you Good God and Allelujah that our beautiful and nappy, fine and beautiful, natural God given hair is not worth it. Our hair is from you and even this we refuse. Hence we refuse you all around. How stupid are we and can we be? We have you because we are made like you and we don't want you. Damn we are truly stupid and ignorant when it comes to self and you. All this money we spend on fakeness – to be fake but yet can't do right and good; positive and clean by our African own.

All these millions we have and all some can do is buy whores, gold diggers that are not worth it. Gold diggers that are riding and hiding with someone else, but yet they see Africa and how Africa has been demonized, looked upon vile as well as being raped of everything. But yet they do nothing about it. It's not their concern hence they stand on the sidelines and watch their African Brothers and Sisters being destroyed whilst those that say they are there to help take everything from them – their African own; home.

As I sit here Good God and write, I am bleeping angry with you and at you to have made us your own. We've become ignorant and stupid, educated fools that know not our true history – life story; roots.

We are not worthy of you hence we cannot help our own and I am bleeping mad. We refuse to truly help but yet say we are Africans. **Well bleep the black race and no wonder other races say we are shit – the filth that they pass from their ass.** *No wonder other races say we are down on the totem pole and food chain.*

We are not blacks because to be Black means to be proud.
To be black means to walk in righteousness and integrity.

To be black means to walk upright and true.
To be black is true love hence we are rare because true love is within us.

We are not blacks because to be black means to truly love your own and truly help your own.

To be black means to be of goodness and truth – true life.
To be black means to be of Good God and Allelujah.
To be black is ALL because ALL is within us All.
All that is good and true is within us but yet we forget this.

I guess over the centuries we've forgotten our blackness – truth. Hence we neglect our true own. No wonder we are the way we are; broken and ruined; not the same.

We've taken up savage ways hence we've become like savages, the less educated, weak and dumb. Instead of building our own, we would rather rape land and people of all.

We would rather lose it all and wallow in dung like scavengers looking for a piece of rotten and or dead meat. We have no shame of self and culture, hence we know not our culture; knowledge of our true own and home.

We are no longer educators that came from the order of God. Instead we've become clowns playing and dancing for the devil for a piece of dry bread – his left over meat of the dead.

We've forgotten about the Exodus. Instead of returning home and building home (Africa) our true mother prosperously, we neglect her and squander all our riches in lands that truly don't like us – truly hate us.

Many don't want us in their lands and instead of getting out, learn from the adage where no dogs are invited, no bones are provided; we fight to stay in these lands and be ridiculed even killed savagely. We complain about these lands so get the hell out. This is what he Good God wants; need.

We are humiliated and killed like animals in these lands but yet we have no ambition and shame to get out – truly leave. They don't want us in their lands, go back to your homeland and build your land prosperously and positively. We are not slaves, we are children of God; but yet in all that he Good God has tried, he's failed with us because we keep telling him we do not want or need him. We keep accepting the devil's own. We would rather fight and build lands that don't want us instead of fighting to build our own in goodness and truth without violence, hate and strife – greed.

We would rather be the degenerates and have nots of Western societies rather than go home to Africa – Mama and invest in our resources – her.

Yes I am pissed at my own black race because we've become the p*****s of so called modern day society. Rather than sustaining ourselves and rise back up to our kingly and queenly status where no one can question us or take our rights from us ever again, we refuse to, hence refusing the call of Mama Africa – Good God and Allelujah.

Instead of being wise, we made them fool us and teach us their wicked and crooked systems – dirty ways. (Bob Marley – Babylon System)

Instead of being wise and thinking wise, we've become fools like them. Fools that seek dominance and control whist putting our God – the God of Truth and Life to shame.

Instead of being wise, we would rather lose it all for a place in hell to burn like them – become extinct spiritually and physically like them.

Instead of being wise and keeping our truth – our heritage, we would rather give it up and adopt their stinking and dirty ways. Ways that was never prescribed by Good God and Allelujah for us to walk, talk and live in.

We know the history and story of Eve and instead of breaking the chain and chains of lies - physical, mental and spiritual slavery, we continue to walk foolishly like Eve – Adam and Eve.

We're not black anymore because we've become the dung of the earth where every race on the face of the planet class us as apes, shit, uncivilized, uncultured, uneducated including our pathetic and sell out own.

We are not treated as humans but yet in all of this, every nation is looking for Jesus (a black man according to Revelations) to save them.

Now tell me this Good God and Allelujah, how can a Black Man, a Black God save humanity when humanity hates his own including his own Black Father, Black God?

Michelle Jean
September 13, 26 and 29, 2014

Oh Lord what a day because it has been eventful.

It's weird because I've been pumping the LIFE WE LIVE by Jah Cure each and every day. I truly love this song and for me to be constantly going to this song is not truly like me. When I am done with a song I don't really go back to it and play it, but this song does something to me. What, I truly do not know.

But then again I am weird.

Truly love the beat hence I can dance to it at will and rock to it when I am writing these books.

Yes I love the way he (Jah Cure) makes reference to Bob Marley. You know Good God, Bob Marley's work and works will stand the test of time. He did educate his listeners before he died. It's a pity his people who are my people could not comprehend him, what he was trying to tell them; teach them. It's a pity they (his people) know not unity nor can comprehend, understand and over stand unity. They lack knowledge hence the devil fool them with his bag of tricks all the time.

Music is great hence I have to connect with you Good God. I have to connect with your mysticism - truth of all.

Yes I am seeing more and more and it's weird now but I am seeing ghost (the dead) in daylight. I mean I am use to seeing dead people in my dreams and when I close my eyes, but to see them and or glimpse them more in the living with my naked eye is something else. Oh well maybe next time she will show me her face instead of her black dress.

Yes to human standards I am not normal because I can see death but hey this is me. There is nothing tricky about it. This is natural and normal for me. I don't know if I will ever stand before a dead man or woman (ghost) and talk to them just like that like some people, but maybe one day. Will it be scary? I hope not.

Dear God what would I say to him or her?

But what a Lala. I am talking about ghosts and talking to ghosts - the dead. Well what about you?

Why can't I see you and talk to you face to face in the living?

What would I say to you?

Dear Lord you are in trouble now because I would crazy glue me to you and talk to you until you get sick of me.

Yes the weirdness is coming out and I had better leave things alone because I will so get off track like I am now. Yes this is the normal me. Always off track hence I truly do not think in the box like some of you and or other humans do.

I have to do things differently, think differently and stand differently.

Damn I have to go back to flirting and desiring my true loved ones - true readers and FAM; family of these books.

We are due for a dinner and music date and now the stupid internet isn't working for me to truly blow your mind away with my musical selections - choices.

See, no fair because the candles have to do some of the talking and romancing for me.

Soon my true loved ones, soon because I so have to talk and be with the lots of you.

Will I get perverted?

Want to but my perverted is not your perverted. My perversion is mild compared to some of you. Don't want to cross the boundaries with porn.

Truly don't want to go there because I so cannot comprehend how some women can do this for a living. Sleeping with a different man each and every day. Yes the pleasure is nice but does it not get boring to be doing the same thing day in and day out? I guess it takes a special kind and type of love to keep going.

I guess you have to be a sex addict to appreciate this industry and be in this industry of immorality in regards to men and women defiling self and living in sin. Yes sexual intercourse is great but there is a fine line to walk when it comes to clean and unclean – true perversion that is governed and enjoyed by demons. Hence sexual intercourse is important to the existence of sin and man – humanity. Given the right circumstances we will find pleasure elsewhere and we do. We do not think of the consequences as sex is both good and bad depending on how it is had, thought of and done. Many are weak and some are just addicts – addicted to sex and this is sad because there is beauty in lying with your lifetime partner; your one and only. Unity is great but one cannot be weak and the other strong. And yes you can say this is a double standard and hypocritical stance on my part given my novel Bodaciously You.

Ah well to each his and her own I guess. Hence the different type of porn. Soft porn, hardcore. And I will not talk about the rest because many humans in this world have and has literally gone mad; sick in the head – mind. Hence their sexual preference of a different kind.

Is this industry safe?

I say not because of the abuse that goes on. The sexually transmitted diseases that are caught - had. Your life is not the same, hence the many deaths of porn stars from suicide, heroin, steroids, alcohol; rape and low self esteem.

This world is not pretty behind the scenes but you have to give it to these girls because they are doing their thing no matter how morally wrong this is. But I am not here to judge anyone morally or ethically. A job is a job no matter how painful and shameful it is. Life goes on but for those that have chosen immorality life ends. You die, hence you have not a beginning; but you surely have an ending.

Michelle Jean
September 13, 2014

As summer comes to close I truly have to wonder Good God.
Wonder what's going to happen to me and you
Our true relationship
Spiritual being

I still can't get over the fact that you, not me, you let our beautiful flowers wither and die.

Now I have to wonder if this is the end of us, me and you.
You and me

It's like how can you make true love die?
How can you not comprehend truth - true love?

Are you like man that cannot handle the abundance of truth you are given?

Could you not comprehend the scope of my truth when it comes to you?

So then I ask you, are you the false one? Because you did make our flowers wither and die.

Are you the false angel that lurks in the dark that was hoping to win at something and failed? Did you think I would back down from my truths - true love of you? So now you can't handle me you've let go; let us come to an end in this way?

Truth is absolute Good God as well as unconditional. It cannot die but with you truth can fade, wither and die because you are not truth, nor can you comprehend it; live it truthfully. The greatest thing a person can have is truth - true love because true love cannot and will never ever hurt anyone but with you, you can hurt, hence now I have to question your truth yet again and this is truly not right on our part, it is wrong. Wrong on your part because you are the one to let the flowers I gave to you out of true and unconditional love; joy wither and die.

I did not make our flowers wither in your world, you did.
The devil did not make our flowers wither
My guides and angels did not make our flowers wither
My gorgeous and beautiful mother did not make our flowers wither

YOU ALONE MADE OUR FLOWERS WITHER AND DIE.

You alone did me wrong.
You alone was the unjust and untruthful one.
You alone came with conditions and stipulations I knew nothing about.

SO NOW THE QUESTION I ASK YOU IS, WHEN ARE YOU GOING TO TRULY GROW POSITIVELY WITH ME AND PLANT FLOWERS FOR ME AND YOU THAT CANNOT FADE AND WITHER; DIE?
Do you want to lose me Good God?
Do you truly want to lose me?

Were you justified in letting our flowers - the flowers I gave to you out of truth, true and unconditional love wither and die?

Are you saying you are dead to me?
Are you saying you don't truly love me?
Are you saying you don't appreciate the flowers I gave to you?

Are you saying if I go to Luxembourg I am dead to you?

All that I do for you, you would make wither and die?

But how can this be when you are my every day and forever ever truth and everything?

True love cannot fade and wither; die when it comes to me and you. But with you it's a different story – matter.

So now I ask you this, if you did not want me to buy you store bought flowers, why did you not tell me face to face?

Why do you not raise me up so that I can have my own piece of land where I can and will make you a rose garden of truth and unconditional love? We will have herbs and spices, breadfruit and jackfruit trees, coconut and mango trees too.

We will have all we need and want that will bring us true joy and happiness – true peace and unity.

I truly love nature and I know you do too. But truly let nothing of ours fade; wither; die ever again. I refuse death so truly do not do this again lest I be severely angry at you.

Beauty is in my eyes for you and if you cannot comprehend my beauty and truth when it comes to you, then you cannot comprehend anything nor can you comprehend me. I refuse to fight with you and be in a war with you. No. I will calm my temper with you. Hence I will not fight with you like I've said. No, black flowers (roses) will not do. Too dark and you know me and darkness. Can't find the beauty in total darkness because I cannot see with my own eyes freely. The person have to come out of the darkness for me to see them hence I am so lost at times. I am seeing white men in total darkness wanting to have sex with me and this is not normal for me. No for real Good God. When did white men start coming into the darkness and how come I have not seen them in this way before? Strange but this is my reality I guess when it comes to me and my sight. I am constantly learning in bits and pieces instead of whole. White Men are just like Black Men when it comes to the darkness hence I am so going to leave well enough alone. So when you white people cuss black people I am now going to laugh because just as how black men are unseen in the darkness you are unseen too. There is no difference in the race in this sense. And I am not expecting humanity to comprehend this because this is shocking in a way to me but it shouldn't be. I'm just on the white level I guess - the second level of life that house another race to the eye. That which is the white race – the Sikh (sick) people of old. So yes your history and heritage was stolen from you. Hence welcome to the Black World where thieves steal what truly belong to us and say it is theirs – their own.

No Good God I cannot find beauty in the dark, hence I do not fully comprehend the dark nor can see through the dark properly sometimes. However, you are my Blue and White everything and then some. So truly enjoy me on the day and days I go buck wild for you.

So if you cannot comprehend my beauty and truth, then you are not the creator nor did you create all. There is more than an abundance of truth and true love in me for you and if you cannot latch on to this abundance then what say you? Something must be wrong then but not with me but with you. As God - Good God you cannot discard me just like that come on now.

What did I do to you?

No, don't answer that but discard this question because I know what I did.

God - Good God I cannot talk to you anymore about goodness and truth. My existence isn't based on lies nor should you base your existence on lies. I refuse lies and so should you. Life - true life is truth and if you as Good God and Allelujah cannot comprehend this, then you truly have nothing and will have nothing. And yes I will leave you. One cannot give in truth truthfully and the other return all in lies - untruth. This is wrong, come on now.

There are no guilt and guilt trips in our world, so truly hold on because our ride and life is not a bumpy one. No, it is in some way because I have to be teaching you about truth and true love; me.

If you don't want to share me with anyone then say so. You and I know I cannot stay lonely all the days of my life. I need to interact with people and do things with them.

Yes I truly love it when your jealousy runs but what I give to you in truth should not have to pay the price for your jealousy. When you let these flowers fade, wither and die, then you are telling me I am dead to you and you want nothing from me.

You are telling me you do not want or need my true love and this cannot be.

You are given truth and true love by me and you are telling me you don't want it. You are going to let my truth and true love die when it comes to you. So what good am I to you if you do this?

Why write these books for you if you are letting my flowers wither – our flowers of truth wither and die?

What purpose do I serve to you when you let my flowers of truth to you die?

What you are telling me is that you are miserable and you cannot handle truth. You would rather truth wither and die before you let it live and grow up in beauty and truth.

You are telling me you cannot handle the true beauty of unconditional love.

I don't know Good God when it comes to you and certain things anymore.

I am glad you are jealous but you cannot allow truth and true love to die. You cannot take your anger out on what I give to you in truth. You are not death nor are you dead. You are life and we have to take care of it; share. You are getting truth and true love hold on to it. Why kill it? Are you death now? If you are, when did you become death? Come on now.

You want us to truly love and respect you and when you get this true love you can't handle it. Say you don't want it. So if this is the case why bother with man?

Why bother with me?

Why bother with humanity? And why the hell should we bother with you?

You can't handle my truth then don't want any of us in humanity to truly love you. Because if you can't handle me, how the hell are you going to handle them and their truths - true love? And yes I am pointing at your true people.

Don't say you need someone and or us to be truthful and honest with you, then turn around and sin everyone if the one thing you are getting you are going to allow to die and or can't handle. You are giving and spreading false hope. Hence I told you, I refuse to tell people to join you and or truly love you; choose you. You are our right hence you should be our choice on any given day. Come on now. You are getting true love and don't want it. Can't handle it.

Are you dumb or just plain out stupid?

No Good God I have to go there, so truly forgive me when it comes to my harshness with you. But do you know how good and wonderful it is to be truly loved by someone including good and true spirits?

Do not let our true love fade because if you do, you will have nothing and that's a crying shame. You cannot be disobedient like us come on now.

Someone loves you true unconditionally beyond any known universe and is doing all to make you happy, take the goodness and truth of true love and make both your lives fulfilled and happy. Make the next person's life easier because they are trying to make yours easier too. I'm trying to ease your burden, so truly accept me as I truly accept you. It's not hurt for hurt but everlasting and forever ever truth when it comes to me and you. Listen, I know you are not use to me and my craziness and don't you dare say, ya think. You have someone that truly loves you; enjoy the truth she is giving you because you and I know just how rare true and unconditional love is. You and I know true love does not come along each and every day hence the rareness of it. So enjoy and cherish the truth I am giving you. Come on now.

Look at life Good God. How long has it been since true love came your way?

A long time right?

Yes you say.

So enjoy me and don't be stubborn come on now.

You are like a yoyo now in the true love department. Your love and or loving us so is truly not truthful is it? You can't handle true love admit it?

You don't know what it's like to be truly loved until now and you can't handle it; Me.

You don't know the rareness of it hence the light in me is not in you. Come on now.

Good God take my hand and feel the truth - true love in me for you. Put your hands on my belly and absorb it because this truth and true love lies in the womb. My womb; hence the womb is the giver and receiver of life. You are a part of my womb hence I do not love you so, I love you true, unconditionally.

Feel the warmth in me and let this warmth light up your world forever ever because it is true, that which I truly give to you infinitely and indefinitely forever ever without end unconditionally.

Grow and glow with me in truth. Never let us fade because if you do, you will be lost not just to me but to your true and good people - the universe. Our true love is rare; truly don't let it go for anything or anyone.

Enjoy and grow, continue to grow up positively and truthfully.

So prosper with me in truth and true love.
Prosper with me in life and all the goodness of life and the true universe.
Prosper with me in all we do that is good and true for each other and others.

Life - good life is clean and enjoyable, so truly enjoy life with me. Yes I will get crazy but that's me. Me Michelle.

Take my hand because you know I truly love to go shopping with you. So let's continue to do good and well for each other and others indefinitely unconditionally.

Hope is in me and it is in you too. So let's be each others hope indefinitely continuously.
You are a part of my good and true world, so truly don't let us lose each other nor lose sight of each other.

So as Good God and Allelujah, plant a good and true tree for us, the both of us. This tree cannot wither, it must stand the test of time indefinitely without end because we, you and me (I) truly cannot end. We are unconditional, unconditional love; true love.

My goodness is your goodness and you know this.

My thoughts are your thoughts, so why do you truly want to divorce me?

If there is darkness in me that is vile truly help me to rid my thoughts and world of it.
Truly be there for me and let us, our true love continue to grow and glow in unison forever ever without end.

Do not cause me anymore tears because I am causing you none. And if I am, I need you to tell me right away.

I need you to be in the midst of all that I do and think. So nothing evil and vile should come from me and you. We are truth - true truth remember. We are unconditional.

Yes I know I have to remind you of this sometimes but I should not have to all the time.

I am a hand holder and you know I truly love to hold on to you because I am secure. But as a human, I need to huddle and cuddle. I cannot go on needing intimacy because the spirit needs it from time to time and you know this.

Remember I tell you everything. Hence I am more than clingy to you. You know I cannot afford to lose you but you have to recognize my sexual needs and wants too. I am now at that stage where I want and need to explore my sexual desires, but I truly don't want to explore it and or be intimate with any and anyone. I need you to ordain that right person that we, me and you are going to be happy with; enjoy.

I truly do not want or need someone that is going to take me away from you and our spirituality either.

Good God I truly do not need false hope because I rely on you for everything good and true. If you cannot give me everything good and true, then what good are you to me or anyone?

You are our lighthouse and beacon and I need this forever ever with you. If you know someone and or the one I choose is going to take me from you then don't ordain the union – relationship; person. I truly cannot afford to lose you and I keep telling you this but you don't listen and when wi gaane now you a halla sey wi ungrateful.

Yu quarrel sey wi nuh listen.
Yu quarrel sey wi nuh loyal and truthful to you.

But are you loyal and truthful to us?

Do you truly listen to us?

Remember you hurt and you only love us so. Therefore, I have to ask you these questions because some of us are trying to be faithful but you are the unfaithful one. Instead of truly calming the storm and easing us out of the pressures of wicked and evil people, you keep us in places we truly do not want to be in.

You let harm come our way, whether that harm be physical, spiritual, mental, health wise, financial, starvation; death. Yes I know you and I trust in you but does it truly have to be this way? Yes I fully comprehend, understand and over stand but the pain is too great for many of us.

Yes the pain and hurt make us stronger but truly is pain and hurt the right way? The suffering is there because many do not make it and in many ways you are to blame. We can blame you but we truly can't because we are the disobedient ones. But I blame you anyway because I can. And this is because I truly love you and know you.

I know you are fed up of us not listening to you, but Good God listening isn't a one way affair and or union. Listening is a collective; go both ways. Hence we are to listen to each other. We are to hear what the next person is saying and do what we can to not create strife and or hurt and pain to the next person. We are not to hurt period but yet we hurt anyway including you.

I cannot do all the listening and you are heading for another route and or heading in another direction – the wrong direction. This cannot work. We have to solve the issues that are plaguing us so that others do not come and make the same mistakes. They must be able to learn from these issues and keep the peace indefinitely and forever ever once we have come to the right and truthful decisions that's going to carry us through for lifetimes and generations to come. Come on now

I cannot give truth and you give false because truth cannot be imbalance, it can only be balanced all the time.

Truth cannot die because the truth is life, everlasting life. Good life cannot die, it can only grow up to you and you know this.

You cannot say you need the truth and expect lies to be given to you. This is not going to work so learn to listen. Not because you are God; the supreme. As parents we have to learn to listen to our children and you are one to not do this; listen. Eee come eene like tick pap inna you ease hole. And I've told you this already.

And don't you dare suck yu teeth an fold yu han at me. You are not a child so truly listen. Yes many of us are disobedient but if father cannot listen, how the hell do you expect children to listen and do right by you - obey?

You need to grow up and know that your children are going to want to experience something new. I want and need to. But if my wanting and needing to experience something new is going to cause you heartache and pain, I won't do it. Like Luxemburg. I won't go because you don't want me to go and I've told you this above. So if I am listening to you, why can't you truly listen to me; others?

Why can't you truly do right by me; others?

We should not have to leave each other because death is not my road and it should not be yours either. Come on now.

Let's talk Good God because I am truly going to talk to you. Oh man how do I begin?

You know what. I was going to talk about White Jesus in this book, but I am going to let him go and put White Jesus in the book What A Mess. And if I don't put him in What A Mess, I will find a way to put him in another book if you permit me to do so. I don't know when I will get it done but hopefully soon.

I have a lot to do and I am hoping to get our house - your mega mansion so that I can truly be at rest and true peace with you. So in all that you do please open good and true doors for us because you are truly important to me.

Michelle Jean

So for all the pain we've caused each other we truly need to heal and stop.

We need to put our hurt and pain behind us and start anew – fresh.

You Good God is our message and hope.
You are our God of Truth and we do truly need you.

You are our fixer and healer
You are our way
You are our everything because without you we would all be dead – nothing.

Yes I know many are dead and walking as the dead but with all that said, we are kneeling at your footstep for a saving grace.

We are knocking down your door for a saving grace.
We are calling out to you despite our wrongs.

Listen Lovey, I do not need your promises; I need your word and words of truth to get me by.
I need your word and words of truth to save me.

Heal all that is wrong with me mentally, physically (heart wise) and spiritually.

I do not put my trust in man; I put all my trust in you because you are there with me in the storms that come my way. So why should I let you go for anyone or anything?

Why should I be ungrateful to you?

You are my goodness and despite my ups and downs, I refuse to go to someone else with my problems. I truly have you and you are my all and king. So why should I break you down? Why should I break your trust?

You are lifting me up and calming the storms, so why should I not lift you up and calm your storms as well? Why should I turn from you when I am more than determined to join you and be with you in goodness and in truth?

Why should I turn from you when everything is starting to pick up and be okay for me and with me?

Hell has nothing to offer me, so why should I give you up for false hope; hell and death?

When I do this, then I would not have truly loved you.

So no matter my storms, I can't give you up because I am up with you. I must grow up and glow with you in every way and or in all that I do in goodness and truth for you and of you as well as others.

Yes it's hard at times but the hardness is dissipating. Look Good God, I am going to travel soon because you made a way for me to do this. So why should I give you up or even give up on you? Yes I am hurt by the flowers, hence I ask you truthfully to mend what is broken between us in goodness and in truth positively.

If I am broken in your eyes truly help me to fix me so that you can be proud of me again. Help me to fix me so that you can hold your head up high again. You know when it comes to me and you I truly don't want to be broken nor do I want and need to cause you pain. I truly love you to no end, so why would I want and need to intentionally hurt you and cause you pain; grief?

You are my resources of all that is good and true. So let's heal each other and come together in true truth once again so that we can never be rocked or be broken ever again.

Please, if I have caused you tears let me dry them with my truth forever ever.

I don't need you to hurt anymore, so take my hand and let's truly pray together because I truly need you beside me and with me.

I need all of you hence let's heal us, all of us together.

Touch me as I now touch you in goodness and in truth so that all can be good and well with us and between us.

Let me receive your healing and truth as you receive my healing and truth; goodness and positive energy.

Know that I more than truly love you unconditionally and it is not my intention to hurt you. So as I learn and grow, please forgive me for all the pain and hurt I've cause you in my lifetime and lifetimes to come.

Michelle

Things are changing and before I continue to go on, I have to get into these confusing dreams.

Dreamt I was at a concert in the park. No not park but this forest area that had green trees. The area was beautiful because nature was green and calm. Hence I truly love nature, truly love to see the tall green trees.

In the dream a male friend that I knew was signing and I joined in with the singing. People my voice was lovely. Truly lovely but you know in reality I cannot sing for beans. I am horrid - awful at singing. But in the dream my voice was truly lovely. So I joined in with him while he was singing on stage. I can't remember if I was on stage with him but I was singing with him. After he had finished singing he joined me up on a hill but it wasn't a hill. We were far from the stage area and his arms were around me. He was hugging me. There were female singers but I did not take in their show. This one female singer, dark female passed us and was going home. At the show her mate (could be husband) and child was there. Once the female singer left, her husband and or boyfriend and or mate abandoned the child. He was walking in the woods and instead of holding his son's hand he did not. Hence he was going in one direction and the child went in the other. People the man did not care for his son. Did not care if his son was lost or if someone took him; stole him. When I saw this I panicked and wanted to go to get the child because the little boy was going deep into the woods. But to my relief another black female found the child and directed him on the right path to find his father. And still after that the man did not hold the child's hand. He let the little boy who is no more than 2 - 5 years of age walk by himself while he (the father) was gone again. This is so sad because all he wanted was for the black singer to leave so he can leave the child alone. I don't know people because this is weird hence the singer Keisha Cole came to mind. Don't ask me why her name and face is stuck in my head. The dream did not stop there either. *After all that happened because it was all black people in the forest. I saw this lady cooking flat bread on a coal stove. Outdoor coal stove as in the outdoor coal stoves we Jamaican's use. Like I said, this lady was baking and or cooking bread on it. Flat bread that was expanding and all of a sudden this bear came out of nowhere and ate all the flat bread on the stove. You could see the fire in the stove but it did not matter to the bear, he went into the fire and ate the bread without getting burnt. After that happened, someone else put flat bread to be baked and or cooked and all you could see is the bread rising and widening out; expanding. It was a beautiful sight. So Russia because I am using symbolism here. Whatever you are planning to do with black people and or your next door neighbour Ukraine, squash it because it is not necessary. Peace - true peace is the answer, so stop the nonsense with Ukraine. Hence I am asking peace to be still and squash all the problems between the two nations. Russia, remember Ukraine had one devastating disaster that caused thousands to abandon their homes. Homes they can never return to, so truly do the right thing and truly let peace reign. Do not escalate a fight/war if you of yourself and the Ukraine can avoid conflict. Learn from the old/past because control and dominance is for the weak. Weak men and women dominate and control – exert power because he Good God and Allelujah did not put anyone on the face of this planet to control and dominate anyone – make the next man and woman including child miserable. Power and control does not make anyone strong. Bullies try to control and dominate, conquer whilst making the lives of others miserable. You cause them to live in fear and this is wrong. No one came into this world to be bullied and controlled; dominated. Come on now. When you bully your people and others they learn to hate you and do hate you. And trust me none is looked upon favorably by God – Good God. Know that there is food there for everyone but you Russia cannot be greedy. Share because the Ukraine was once a part of Russia and its communist state. They separated from you hence truly leave them alone. And you Ukraine know who your family is. You cannot spread hate against Russia because you're both each other's keeper. Know that no one can be punished for the good they do, they can only be punished for the evils and wrongs that they do, so truly learn and heal; forgive but never forget. Both lands must begin to trust again. As for you Russia, you are being warned from and by the Most High God – the Supreme Being that created the heaven and earth because somehow he wants good for you hence look after Russia and your people. Because at the end of the day you will be affected by the harvest that's to come. Do now for your people because not everyone will survive this harvest. Hence billions will be lost. So truly get your act together and preserve your people. Start planting and store up food for your people. You know the end hence prepare for the beginning and you will be saved. The world is on high alert as it is already and death isn't dicking around when it comes to humanity. Death is here and it is only going to get worse because humanity including governments have given themselves over to death. We are virtually all doomed. Hence the oil and fortune many of us have and has amassed will be lost. According to man and his statistics there are over seven billion people on earth. Soon that seven billion will turn into just a bit over one hundred and forty four million. Do the math because if you are not a part of Good God's true kingdom then you are doomed - dead. Death must take you by any means necessary. Thus saith the Lord thy God meaning it is so. So truly think and do that which is right. Prepare yourself because Good God and Allelujah is giving you a chance to do right right now so truly know what you are doing.*

Like I said, I am having strange dreams as of late and it cannot be helped because he Good God and Allelujah is trying to tell me something and whatever that something is, I have to try and figure it out. For me I used symbolism with the bear in the dream above but you don't have to. So if you know what this dream means let me know. I'm on twitter at MichelleJean77.

My email address is michellejeanbooks@gmail.com.

Hey those are the two avenues that you can reach me at. Please note: I rarely tweet and or go on twitter. So if you do not get a follow back on twitter please do not feel anyway. Hopefully I will get a postal box soon and you can send me your letters via this route. And please, if you are going to send germicides and or chemicals to end my life, truly don't. Your shit is not needed. Yes you can disagree with me but the death bullshit, keep it to your damned self. I am not about death but life.

Not because you are dead does it mean I want to die with you or by you. So death is truly warned to keep his and her pouches under lock and key. I am not dicking around either because where no bones are provided no dogs are invited. So death, keep your swines of death on your leash and truly leave me the hell alone.

Had to get that in.

Onwards I go because I've strayed.

Also dreamt, I was back in the past. I was in the city of scrolls - the city of life then. This is what I call this land. All black people resided in the land as far as I can see. But with all I saw, I saw the city being destroyed and consumed by fire. One scroll was saved hence I call this scroll, the scroll of life. People wanted this and or these scrolls I guess but they did not get them so they burned and destroyed the city. Weird yes hence Italy comes to mind. Maybe Italy is going to be destroyed and or sink. Some say the Vatican has the ancient scrolls but in truth the Vatican has not the scroll and scrolls of life. Could never have them. Before they get these tablets and or ancient truths all will be destroyed. So to all the lands that have the ancient scrolls please watch out as well as be mindful of your enemies because destruction comes and you truly don't know it.

__The Scrolls of Life is not for wicked and evil people - men and woman to handle. No one, absolutely no one that is wicked and evil – unclean, can touch and or read these scrolls. Like I said, before this happens all will be destroyed and I guess to a certain length or extent this is what has happened thousands of years ago. Hence Bob Marley told us "Jah would never give his power to a bald head." Yes wicked and evil people.__

So somewhere a city is going to be destroyed and or sink in this day and time.

As for children, I keep seeing them. Keep seeing children, young children and it is not pretty.

__I dreamt young babies, children was in this area. Black children - young babies and or children and they were in dirty water. The water was polluted so I truly do not know if there is going to be an outbreak that affects children - black children globally. So Africa truly be on the alert and guard your children and or child population. Maybe a new disease that target black kids will be introduced globally to further kill the black population so truly be on your guard because something is not right. Sin has and have gotten to our children and this is crying shame. Sin should not get to our children hence mothers if you know you cannot afford to have children do not have unprotected sex. Do not have none – any children.__

Do not have unnecessary children you cannot afford because this is a sin, a grave sin.

Know that men are not always going to be around to help us raise our children. Hence we are to bare the pain in raising them (our children) alone and this is happening today. Hence the single parents globally. Men were to leave the nest and this is sad because no child is to be left alone. Children are precious in the eyes of God – Good God hence they are cherished by him.

Some dad's abandon their duty and this is wrong. But it's their waterloo. They must answer to Good God for abandoning life - their children real soon. Hence billions of men will not be saved in the end because they have no good family values and morals nor do they care about their children. Many want to have kids and when they do get them; they abandon the woman and leave them (the woman) alone to bare the burden of raising their children alone.

Hence I refuse to worry about dead beat fathers that care not for their own. They are not a part of Good God's world and can never be a part of mine. As parents we have an obligation and duty to our children. We are to raise them right so that they can grow up to be good and positive citizens that contribute positively to society - life globally.

No people, mama raised children alone and when children and or child grow up and become someone successful and positive, daddy come a running saying my child and or children. Daddy all of a sudden shows up expecting child and or children to help and support him. No. It does not work that way and will never work that way. Child and or children is not obligated to you, that child and or children is obligated to mother and or the stepfather and or stepmother, including good grandmother and father that raised them. YOU ABANDONED YOUR DUTY AND ROLL TO LIFE - YOUR CHILD, HENCE YOUR CHILD AND OR CHILDREN ARE NOT OBLIGATED TO YOU. YOU GAVE UP YOUR PARENTAL RIGHTS TO THAT CHILD AND OR YOUR CHILDREN, SO WHEN THAT CHILD AND OR CHILDREN GROW UP AND GLOW THEN WANT NOTHING FROM THEM BECAUSE THEY ARE TRULY NOT YOUR OWN. THEY BELONG TO SOMEONE ELSE AND IT IS THAT SOMEONE ELSE THAT RAISED THEM THEY ARE OBLIGATED TO AND NOT YOU. This is the law and it cannot be changed to suit and please you. And don't you dare say it's the mother's fault because a good woman will never stop a child's father from participating in their child's life. Come on now. Stop the blame game and grow up. Yes if you are abusive to your child then she has and have all rights to protect that child from you. Come on now.

Trust me on this. God - Good God and Allelujah will not hold that child and or children with sin. You the father and mother that have and has neglected your child and or children is the one to be held in contempt; accountable. You abandoned your duties as a parent and caused your child and or children pain and suffering. This is why you are told, Good God's people are children. When you as a parent make a child suffer, you are causing Good God and Allelujah pain and suffering. You are causing Good God and Allelujah to suffer because you are taking away his true goodness from that child.

So to some of you deadbeat (dead) fathers, truly good luck because *YOUR WOES HAVE BEEN SOUNDED BY ME. YOUR TRUMPET BLOWS AND SOUND. SO TRULY WOE BE UNTO YOU BECAUSE YOU HAVE BEEN FOUND GUILTY OF SIN BY ME AND GOOD GOD LITERALLY. Thus saith the Lord thy God meaning it is so. You do not abandon your duties to life - your children. You do not allow others to abuse them or look down upon them. (Your child and or children).*

You do not sell them (your children) as sex slaves - whores and prostitutes.
No child begged you to have them. You laid with your mate and had them and your responsibility as a father and mother is to take care of them (your child and or children) and raise them right, good and well.

You cannot say you are a father and shun your responsibility. Hence I say to the youths yet again that say if daddy was there they would not do certain things. This is a cop out and this is bullshit on your part. If mother is there, grandparents, aunt and uncles are there struggling to raise you right, hold your head up and be proud because the most important person is there for you in your life. Your aunt or uncle including grandparents is your mother and father. They are the ones to show you true love so be there for them and listen to good council. Do not add to their pain and heartache; stress because at the end of the day, if you lose them you will have nothing.

If you know washing the dishes is your chore then do the dishes without complaint. Show gratitude in a good way. Sometimes if you feel like making your grandparents and or aunt or uncle breakfast, make them breakfast. Help them to lighten their load so that you and them can live prosperously and positively.

I don't care if you sleep on the floor. Keep that floor clean. Make a box and or something of wood to put your clothes in neatly so that it does not have to be on the floor if you can. If you weave with straw; make straw baskets to put your clothes in, but do for you and them positively come on now.

Well I live in the slums and it's not easy. Fine but who made these slums? Was it not nasty people that don't want better for self and the community? Was it not nasty people to throw their garbage every and anywhere instead of thinking of self and the community? Why be dependent on the government when you of your self can clean self and the surroundings that you live in?

As people truly think. The government did not dump garbage in your community. You dumped your garbage in your community. You are the ones that has and have that slum state of mind. You are telling your mind you want to live in these slums. Slums can be changed into a beautiful and clean communities. Will it be easy?

No, because the slum mentality is instilled and engrained in some of the people. Listen it costs nothing to keep your common area clean. It cost's nothing to pick a flower and plant it in your front yard.

If you have a back yard and have beans; it cost nothing to plant those beans. What will cost you is the thieves that will now steal your hard work and labour but don't give up.
If you can afford a can of paint, paint your house. If you weave, make some crazy and funky mats that people will buy and sell those mats. Once you start venture out to the tourist area or sell to shops but be leery of thieves that will rob you. Do not take up arms with them, just continue to pray and everything will be okay. Remember the greatest weapon a trying and good person has is Good God and Allelujah. All that wicked and evil people do to you must and will come to an end – their end if you trust him. So worry not what they do. I am here to plea to Good God for all of you that is good and true to him, self and others including land, the country that you live in; call home. One day better comes but that better depends on you and your goodness – truth. So truly listen to I Understand by Smokie Norful and rely on him Good God no matter how hard and doubtful it becomes. Like you he Good God does hurt. Listen to Smokie when he said, *"Oh one more day, one more step, I'm preparing you all for myself. I'm getting you ready and if you can't hear my voice, if you can't hear me speaking ooh just trust my plan. Yeah I am the Lord I love you, I see you and I understand*

ooh. I am the lord I see what you are going through, every problem, every trial, every burden, every situation. I understand, I won't leave you, yeah, yeah I understand." Trust me Good God is there for all of us who need him. He's waiting on us to truly receive him and stop the nonsense we are doing in our lives. We have to respect him and respect self and if we cannot do this then truly do not ask him for help because he will not be there for you. We cannot do all for death and then turn around and expect Good God to save us. How does this work? God – Good God is not our scapegoat nor is he our pupunennay. Come on now. We have to do better come on now.

All you have to do is continuously pray to him. Talk to God – Good God when you are alone, laying on your bed, sofa; sit on your toilet and talk to Good God. Every chance you have to connect with him connect with him. Make Good God your confidant and friend and he will be there for you. Trust me all that do you evil and try to do you evil he Good God will show you them. Know that their evils and the pain they want for you will return unto to them more than ten folds. So worry not about wicked and evil people. Live your life good and clean because evil hath an end, but life - good and true live hath no end and never will have an end. It cannot end. Evil know that their life is coming to an end soon, so they are doing all to destroy the earth so it cannot be livable. But I am trusting Good God to truly put an end to their plans and schemes. You gave up your life to death willingly, so now that death comes go with death and don't turn to Good God for a saving grace come on now.

I am going to interrupt this book because I went ballistic on Good God this morning. October 1, 2014. I read on the internet George Clooney sold his wedding photos to the highest bidder and the money he gets will go into funding his spy program. His desire is to continue spying on North Sudan.

People I've written about this before in some of my other books, Blind Obsession Rebuttal The Truth Is Now Or Never including others. Hence I am going to get racist. I truly like this guy but the bullshit of him spying on black people has to stop. No black land can spy on America, so why is an American overstepping his authority and boundaries and spying on black people in Africa?

George, I've had to read on the internet someone's nasty comment about the black race. They classed the black race as shit. The filth that comes out of their ass. Yes I've called other gods shit, but I know why I call them that. It is because when evil and wicked people die and or dying in the physical world they emit the odor of shit literally. So I know what I am talking about hence I am justified in calling other gods shit.

Now Sudan, I said my peace above and my true peace stands. As Sud – Sudan you can say I am not of you and I am to bleep off and leave your business alone, but I cannot do this because something is not right. This man is spying on North Sudan and I am against him for this. Hence I am going to get racist and I truly don't give a damn if the world hates me further for it. And this is why I get mad at Good God for sticking with the Black Race because we truly care not for our own. We are a disgrace when it comes to the treatment and help of our own, our own race and people; African people.

Nelson Mandela spent 27 years in jail fighting for his people and his people let him down.

All that he fought for was for naught because you have a bleeping Black Leader that governs South Africa and it's as if he cares not for his people. He refuses to help his own in a true and positive way. I am bleeping tired of everyone belittling and using the black race for their own profit and gossip; personal gain. I'm tired of the black race being the bleeping joke of the world and we are so stupid and ignorant that we refuse to change self for the better and do right for self and our own. We are not bleeping buffoons but yet we keep acting – behaving like one.

NO ONE CAN TELL THE BLACK MAN ABOUT SELF A PART FROM THE BLACK MAN – BLACK RACE. No one can live our life a part from us. Come on now. We have to do better for self instead of looking like people waiting for the what not and leftovers of other races. We are not hungry because we have our god. We have Mother Africa – Good God's land, hence we have food and can plant food to feed our own. We need to stop relying on others now and become self reliant. Dependant on self and all the goodness he Good God has and have given us to maintain and sustain us – self. Great people came from Africa so what happened? Why did we give up our greatness to become lowly slaves (Abdullah); the servants and clowns of man – humanity? Great are we because he Good God resides in us. So please let's return to greatness and hold the hand of Good God forever ever continually.

We are not hopeless because Good God is our hope and life. We are the ones to give him up hence leaving us the black race desperate and destitute; without a home and god.

Now that Tata is gone, it seems Black South Africans have not a home and it's a shame because I know his grief. I see the grief on his face because he showed me him. It's as if he's telling me South Africa is lost, his people have no hope and I refuse to accept this for Black Africans globally including Black South Africans. We cannot be lost because he Good God gave us a home – his life and we keep giving all that he has given us away.

Please my people come home and hold on. Hold on to your king because he does truly love you. He cannot love you so if you are not with him and for him. Come on now.
Like I said, **_I DO NOT WANT WHITE HOPE. I TRULY NEED BLACK HOPE BECAUSE WHITE IS SPIRITUAL DEATH AND IT'S TIME BLACKS GLOBALLY WALK AWAY FROM DEATH._**

IT'S TIME WE ACCEPT GOOD GOD AND LIVE BECAUSE DEATH IS NOT LIFE IT'S DEATH AND WILL FOREVER BE DEATH. WE AS BLACKS NEED TO SMARTEN UP AND GO BEYOND THE NEEDS OF US. WE NEED TO GROW UP AND GLOW IN GOODNESS AND TRUTH FOR ALL OF GOOD GOD'S PEOPLE AND CHILDREN; US.

WE AS BLACKS ARE DOWN NOW BUT WE ARE TRULY NOT LOST BECAUSE GOOD GOD IS WITH US AND WILL FOREVER BE. RELINQUISH THE DEVIL'S WAY AND ACCEPT LIFE'S WAY. THE WAY OF TRUTH, HONESTY, CLEANLINESS, TRUE LOVE, JUSTICE – THE JUST.

As for you George Clooney, I am pissed and I went to Good God to

voice my concern. Let me tell you this, YOU ARE NOT BLACK, YOU ARE WHITE THAT FALL UNDER THE BANNER OF WHITE. A person that truly loves cannot hurt the next man or woman and by you continuing your spy campaign when it comes to NORTH SUDAN you have no good will for Sudanese People. YOU ARE PITTING FAMILY AGAINST FAMILY AND YOU ARE INFINITELY AND INDEFINITELY WRONG. YOU ARE INSTIGATING WAR AND SOUTH SUDAN SHOULD BE INFINITELY AND INDEFINITELY ASHAMED OF SELF AND COUNTRY. You George Clooney is not there to help anyone. You are there for South Sudan's oil but the people and government of South Sudan is too foolish to see this hence they will pay shortly. Thus saith the Lord thy God meaning it is so.

Sud – Sudan is Good God's land because life rests in that land and instead of cherishing the beauty of life Good God has and have given them; they taint it and accept the devil's own.

I truly refuse you George because the people of Sudan is your scapegoat for your hidden agenda.

LIKE I SAID, YOU ARE NOT BLACK HENCE YOU HAVE NO LEGAL AND MORAL RIGHT TO GO INTO BLACK LAND AND SPY ON BLACK PEOPLE. GOOD GOD DID NOT MAKE YOU THE MESSENGER FOR THE SUDANESE PEOPLE OR THE BLACK RACE ON A WHOLE.

GOOD GOD DID NOT TELL YOU TO INTERFERE IN SOMETHING YOU KNOW NOTHING ABOUT.

NORTH AND SOUTH (NOD AND SUD) HAS AND HAVE ALWAYS BEEN IN CONFLICT AND IT'S TIME FOR IT TO END. BUT YOU CANNOT END IT BY PITTING FAMILY AGAINST FAMILY. WAR

Like I've said, you are wrong because you are continuing the strife.

You would not like it if someone spied on you, so who the bleep gave you a white man the right to play the hero for us when you are not the hero but the devil in disguise. Good God did not ordain the devil – a white devil to speak for him. She Adau is to build a school in Sudan. He Good God and Allelujah asked her to do this, so truly step aside and let Good God let his ordained black people do his work. *She Adau is Sudan's saving grace not you.* She's Sudanese hence Good God will not let someone that is not of Sudanese decent save Sudan. The school she's to build she must do it truthfully and clean. Also, she cannot bring religion into this. She has to separate herself from religion and if she does not do this, she will fail. Yes I brought racism into this. Yes this is sad on my part but I will not stand for bullshit when it comes to the devil's race of people. True blacks walk away from strife and evil, so take it as you please because I sick and tired of people saying they are for us (the black race) and with us (the black race) then stab us the black race in the back and take what is rightfully ours. A true black person whether white, black or Chinese work for the better good of the black race and you are not a part of the black race – the banner of Good God and Allelujah hence you are duly warned. And truly ***I don't bleeping care if America put my name on their terror list. America and Americans are worse than terrorists when it comes to the Black Race. They have enslaved and killed us but yet the world is looking at them and following them (America) to their doom. Bleep America because your land is condemned. You are war mongers that exert your authority when no one truly wants you or care for you. You willing invade other lands and kill their people but America's day is coming when all the lives you've taken must be vindicated because the law of God say, "thou shalt not kill" but you kill and destroy anyway. You have no respect for the laws of God nor do you have any respect for your black citizens hence the Southern Cross and or Confederate Flag and Eye in Triangle has been taken from you infinitely and indefinitely without end and handed back to Good God and Allelujah for safe keeping because America and his people have and has become unworthy.*** Know this, the names of every American is firmly engrained in deaths book – the book of the dead. So hear me Good God's children – the Jews – come out of Babylon – modern day Babylon because America is slated to fall and is going to fall. The Exodus is now so truly find your own – home. Yes it's ***OH MY GOD TIME BECAUSE AMERICA HAS AND HAVE BEEN FOUND GUILTY OF SIN – IMMORALITY.*** Your land is worse than Sodom and Gomorrah because when death see sin, death sees the people of your land literally and that is a crying shame. ***When death talks about sin your name, THE UNITED STATES OF AMERICA is called. Not Russia, not Alaska, not Iraq and Iran but America.*** Your land is not what we are to be or become hence you are in sins book – the book of the dead. So death won over your land and it is a matter of time before America pays and pay dearly because soon earth must stop yielding life to man – the wicked and evil of the land globally indefinitely. This time will be worse than Noah because billions are going to see hell and face hell globally on land real soon.

I've told you George in another book to take your spy satellite down because what you are doing is wrong. North and South have to work their differences out in peace and they cannot do it with religion because he Good God and Allelujah did not give his people religions of men to kill self. Do not pit South against North because whether you know it or not, Good God and Allelujah is a Southerner and he does hurt. He does hurt back so truly know what you are doing and stop dicking around with his people. Life rests in Sudan – South Sudan so know what you are doing because what you truly do not want for self do not want it for others. You know not the history of North and South so stop trying to play God because you are not a part of God's race of people from your choice. You chose wrong and it is that wrong choice that will be your family's as well as your downfall.

Yes you may have married a Babylonian – Lebanese and or whatever creed she is. And I give you my word that she is not true because she is Muslim but yet willingly side with you to continue to spy on her Islamic own. Bleeping turn coat and sell out. Hence North Sudan be on your guard and walk away from Islam because no land of God and no child of God is to accept Islam. Islam was our own yes but they the Babylonians that conquered and colonized us more than 24000 years ago polluted our home hence Good God saw it befitting to separate us from them. **_What Good God forbids us to do we are to do. He's forbidden us to go back into Islam and we are to stay away and out of Islam indefinitely. My homeland is dirty and I want to go on vacation there but Good God will not allow me to. He's separating me from wicked and evil – dirty people. So truly learn and redeem yourself with him. Take heed and walk away from death because shortly the harvest comes and many lands will pay. And yes it hurts that I cannot go home but it is not my will but Good God's will. My people failed him and he is protecting me. He's saving me so I have to listen._** Yes Jamaica has a saving grace but it's up to them. They must become 99.9% clean like Lysol but truly good luck with that. Meaning, I have no confidence in them and that's a crying shame on my part. Hence Jonah and the whale. Do not continue to make the same mistakes. The Blue and White Nile is your life so truly maintain and sustain it because if it dries up, all of Africa is doomed; dead. He Good God would have lost all around and you cannot let this happen. Come on now. They (my people) now have to live with the devastating cost of their disobedience shortly and it is truly a shame. Good God separated us from them (the Babylonians) long ago but because of trust, (see Adam and Eve) and trusting their lies we've lost our place with Allelujah and Good God. Hence many African Lands speak Arabic which is taken from their mother's tongue; language – Urdu. Know the bleeping truth and walk as well as live in your integrity. Walk before death and live come on now.

KNOW WITHOUT A SHADOW OF A DOUBT THAT THERE IS NO PLACE IN GOOD GOD'S ABODE FOR ANY MUSLIM. Allah stands for and means the BREATH OF LIFE AND EVERY ISLAMIC KINGDOM HAS AND HAVE TAKEN FROM THE BREATH OF LIFE. They kill and lie to self and humanity saying they are going to paradise when in truth each and every one of them is going to hell. "Thou shalt not kill." You cannot break the laws of God and think you will be respected. Hawwah and or Eve broke the code and law of Good God. She disobeyed him and died. So what say you? We are no different from Eve because each and every day we disobey. So because we disobey – sin, he Good God cannot have anything to do with us nor can he truly help us. To sin means you are making yourself dirty – unclean and the more we sin, it's the further He Good God gets. When we sin we are moving away from Good God and Allelujah. Good God is not dirty, he is clean and he cannot live amongst dirty people because he too will become dirty. This is why he chooses his own to deliver his message.

And the reason why he does this is because we cannot hear him when he speaks.
*We cannot see him hence he must speak to us this way. He can speak to you clearly and he does but like I said, **we cannot hear him. Our vibration – wave lengths are not in tune with him. Hence humanity is listening on the wrong frequency; that which is the frequency of death.**_*

Also know that death and or the devil CANNOT GO UP AGAINST GOOD GOD AND ALLELUJAH. The devil knows he cannot prove Good God wrong. Nor can he the devil go into Good God's Kingdom. Hence humanity have and has been deceived by the Jesus bullshit; lies.

Know this. THE DEVIL DIDN'T SET OUT TO DECEIVE GOD – GOOD GOD AND ALLELUJAH. HE SET OUT TO DECEIVE

MAN AND HE DID AND WON. HE DID DECEIVED MAN – ALL OF HUMANITY AND HE USED RELIGION TO DO IT. REMEMBER GOD – GOOD GOD AND ALLELUJAH CANNOT BE DECEIVED, HENCE THE DEVIL KNOWS NOT GOD – GOOD GOD; BUT HE DOES KNOW MAN. He does aid man in sending man – humanity to hell. Like I said, Good God is clean and he cannot go into places that are dirty. Nor can a dirty man or woman including child go into his home – abode. So Satan could have never resided in Good God's Kingdom for which you call heaven. Satan could have only resided in hell because he's unclean. A liar; dirty. We know that demons walk amongst the living. They do talk with the living. It is man – humanity that do not know the truth, cannot differentiate between good and evil.

Every Islamic country mocks Good God hence no place is provided for them in the kingdom and kingdoms of Good God. And if you doubt me, ASK GOOD GOD FOR YOURSELF AND HE WILL TELL YOU THE TRUTH; that which I am telling you.

He will answer you. *So George, no matter you marrying into the realm of death; terror, suicide bombers; death's own, I give you my word in the living and in death that if anything happens to one Sudanese because of your spy campaign, I will ensure every PERSON OF IRISH DECENT AND EVERY ROMAN CATHOLIC BOTH LIVING AND DEAD GLOBALLY INCLUDING YOUR FAMILY FIND NO PLACE WITH GOOD GOD AND ALLELUJAH INFINITELY AND INDEFINITELY FOREVER EVER WITHOUT END. Whatever it takes to keep every Irish and every Roman Catholic globally out of the abode of Good God and Allelujah I will do. All that has their name in the BOOK OF LIFE RIGHT NOW I will petition Good God to turn them over to death because of what you have done. I also give you my word of truth that NO LEBANESE WILL EVER FIND A PLACE WITH GOOD GOD AND ALLELUJAH BECAUSE I WILL MORE THAN CURSE THEIR ASS INDEFINITELY FOREVER EVER IF SHE DICKS AROUND WITH GOOD GOD'S LAND AND PEOPLE. Know this, the laws of man (Babylon) does not govern Good God's children. We are governed by his laws because we are his people and children. So she had better not pull any of her law and or international law bullshit. She had better not draft up any petition to petition against North Sudan for genocide. America has done worse to blacks hence you had better tell her to keep her Jinny Babylonian deceitful self to herself because America has and have been found guilty. It is just a matter of time before America collapse hence TIME WILL TELL SHORTLY. You cannot charge another race for genocide and crimes against humanity without looking at self – YOUR OWN CONDEMNED COUNTRY AND LAND.*

Remember your American history because Americans fed BLACK BABIES TO GATORS – Alligators.

RIGHT NOW BLACKS ARE BEING SLAUGHTERED LIKE ANIMALS IN AMERICA.

REMEMBER SLAVERY BECAUSE GOOD GOD HAS THESE BOOKS AND SOME INCLUDE PICTURES OF THE ATROCITIES AND EVILS OUR ANCESTORS FACED AT THE HANDS OF AMERICANS. Hence Good God has not forgotten and will never forget the wickedness of Americans towards his own people. America bought and sold black people even slaughtered them like pigs, hence we will never ever forget the evils of America and her evil counterparts that played a part and role in human trafficking – slavery. Trust me hell is there because death hath time to feed now – his time has come when he must feast on his children – his wicked and evil own.

REMEMBER MARCUS MOSIAH GARVEY AND WHAT AMERICA DID TO HIM.

REMEMBER MARTIN LUTHER KING JR AND WHAT AMERICA DID TO HIM.

BLACK PEOPLE HAVE NO RIGHTS IN AMERICA AND YOU KNOW THIS. WE ARE CLASSED LOWER THAN DOGS AND TREATED WORSE THAN DOGS.

So who are you to do this – spy on North Sudan? It's not open season for the slaughter of black people anymore. We need to wake up and do better for self. Hence Bob Marley told us in Ambush in the Night and Babylon System. He told us time will tell and it is telling because all must come to an end shortly. Hence hell is full of people from around the world – globe. Meaning billions have their name in death's book because humans of every race and creed followed the devil and or Satan to their deaths; hell.

Do to help not do to kill because when I petition and curse trust me, it's indefinite and forever ever. Black people are not your game so truly know what you are doing because I refuse to have you hurting a nation of people that has and have done you nothing. Don't bleeping lie to them because if the world does not know it, Good God is on our side and will forever be on our side. It's us as blacks that must walk to him in truth and let go of the devil and his people.

Like I said, you are not black, you are white. A white man that means South Sudan no good because YOU WANT NORTH TO INVADE SOUTH SO THAT AN ALL OUT WAR WILL ENSUE AND IF HE GOOD GOD LETS THIS HAPPEN HE HAS MY WORD THAT I WILL NEVER EVER FORGIVE HIM. I am tired of the bullshit in humanity. So truly hope and pray I am not the saving grace for humanity because the Book of Life is mine and my home. He Good God is mine and I will not let you destroy a beautiful race of people for your own personal gain – oil.

Whites, Blacks and Chinese lived in peace and as one people long ago hence the flag of life – Jamaican Motto say, "OUT OF MANY ONE PEOPLE" and I refuse to let you destroy us because we are black, the people of God – Good God that fall under the banner of Black. Hence we are the true Jews that are from the land of peace – Salem otherwise called

Jerusalem. Not the Jerusalem of Israel – that which is known to modern day man.

Onwards I go because I am truly mad and off track.

No people, blacks are dropping like flies by white cops to further bring race into this. Why the bleep does he not talk to his President and tell him to quell the bullshit and armshouse of the American Police Force.

Death consumes Africa, whites hates Africans and by you spying on a Black Country goes to show me just how worthless the black race has and have become. That we have to have a white man instigate more strive with us so that we die a little more – further.

How would he like it if I put strife between him and his family – friends?
How would he like it if I tell Blacks globally to take up arms against the white race and slaughter them like dogs - animals? ***And no black people we cannot do this; take up arms against white people because "thou shalt not kill." Leave your enemies to time because time does tell in time. This I more than truly know.***

He sure as hell wouldn't, so why is he doing it to the black race?

If you want good for the next man do good and well by them. Do not stir up crap for them to go to war and or for America to invade the land with its NATO counterparts of death to further rape and steal the lands and oil of African People.

Let me ask you this, what right and rights do you have in Africa?
How dare you overstep your authority and boundaries of the black race – people?

African's can't spy on America and Ireland, so who the hell gave you the authority to spy on African land and soil including their people?

Who the bleep died and gave you authority to watch over us – the black man and land – people?

Who died and gave you authority to speak for anyone of us – the black man and land – people?

You are not the savior for Black People so step back and off JUDAS because your lies and deceit is not warranted nor is it wanted and needed. Like I've said, in my other book, Blacks have been raped and abused enough and the lies and deceit must stop. If you cannot help Sudan in a good way, then truly don't help at all. I'm tired of white people coming into Africa waving the White Flag because the white flag represents death and it is death. After you've raped us of everything including dignity you slander us and I will not have it. Life isn't about theft and lies it's about truth – TRUTH FOR ALL.

YOU ARE NOT SUDANESE HOPE. YOU ARE SUDANESE DEATH

BECAUSE YOU SPY ON BLACK PEOPLE; THEM. You knowingly and willingly instigate strife with black people so truly go bleep yourself because you are not one of us. You are Satan in disguise hence you have no good will for Good God's people and that is why you married a Muslim to find favour in Islamic culture; but you will find none. Know that it is unlawful for a Muslim to stand against his or her own. You are on the wrong side bitch. Know this. A Muslim turning against her or his own is like eating pork. You are condemned.

Africa – Sudan do not need white death, they need black hope – truth.

*And no I refuse to insight a race war so anyone say they are going to take up arms against the white race I will commission Good God to take your name and family's name out of the Book of Life infinitely and indefinitely forever ever. I am not dicking around with you either because in truth if we want better we should and must do better for self – ALL. Just as the white race is to blame, the black race is to blame also. We the black race trusted them to have our backs but they stabbed us in it. **Hence we have forgotten that the devil cannot be trusted.** Go back to Adam and Eve in your so called beginning (Genesis) and read the deceit – lies. Not even his own people the devil care about, so what say many of you?*

Like I said, we gave up Good God to accept the devils own. Hence we were told "the wages of sin is death." When we disobey Good God and Allelujah death comes.

When we do not listen to good and true council death comes.
When we do not listen to Good God and Allelujah death comes.
So in many ways we are to blame because of disobedience. Remember Eve did not listen to Good God and she died hence we are no different today.

Good God and Allelujah is trying to protect us but we keep going into the damned fire. Learn to bleeping listen because he Good God bases nothing on colour – colour of skin. Say it so I can tell you to bleep you.

We keep disobeying and dying. Hence despite my racist words, please forgive me because Hue should not come into play but I could not help it due to anger.

I cannot raise up arms against the white race nor will I condone you taking up arms against the white race. I've told you, some whites are black hence they fall under the banner of black – Good God. Some blacks are whites hence they fall under the banner of white – Death and because of this I am telling the black race to put down arms (based on hue) because many of you do not know who you are. I am both of both races hence I can cuss both sides because Good God did not tell me to write for blacks (in hue) alone. Hence know which banner you fall under and one way to do this is to make a check list of your good and evils. If you have more evils than good then you are white – fall under the banner of white – death.

Know that when the messengers of God – Good God and Allelujah condemns you, you are condemned infinitely and indefinitely

forever ever without end. Babylon and the children of Babylon are condemned infinitely and indefinitely forever ever without end hence it is more than forbidden and unlawful to marry any of them. Islam is condemned because they (the Babylonians) polluted our way of life and he Good God saw it befitting to take us out; hence we are not to go back into it (Islam). Islam is worse than Sodom and Gomorrah, so stay the hell out of condemned lands and stay away from condemned people. The true Jews know this but yet refuse to tell you the truth because of fear of the Babylonian Jews. Good God has and have been trying to show us and tell us this for centuries but we as black people refuse to listen hence the harsh punishment comes. When we don't listen he Good God give us over to the sins that we want. Hence he's left us to our pain – sins; nasty will.

No form of religion is of Good God and Allelujah, it is of the devil. Hence we live like devils and wallow in the mess and filth of the devil – demons.

No one can recover from condemnation because your name and number is written in the book of the dead infinitely and indefinitely forever ever. No good that you do can or will save you, so truly take heed humanity.

We say the mark of the beast is 666 but in fact 666 represent the three daughters of Eve. Add another 6 and you will get the true mark of the beast 6666 which is 24. Twenty four thousand years which is one day in spiritual time. Like I've said in a couple of my other books, multiply that number (24 000) by the number of sins you commit each day and or over the course of your lifetime. Then double it and tack on some more time for good measure.

Why double it (your figure)?

Because we are both spiritual and physical beings. Like I've told you, the life you live in the living determines where you go in the afterlife. Meaning when your spirit shed its prison – the flesh.

Know that each sin has a different weight in hell because death made it so and he has a right to because death owns you. Good God cannot interfere with Death because life and death is two different things. We are the ones to choose death over life whilst believing someone is going to die for your sins. No one can die for your sins. Eve believed him and gave up her good up good up life for death and she did not become a God. She became the Mother of death, her children because she did marry death in the living. See your Six Pointed Star. This is true death – the death of all. Yes death's flag. The six pointed star is the seal of death because these people and or the people that fall under this flag are married to death, hence they wrote the Holy Bible; their so called book of lies but yet humanity fail to see this globally. Can't break away from the book of death and lies; deceit.

For example, let's say the weight of adultery is 24000 years in hell. Say for 7 years you've been in an adulterous relationship that you did not get forgiveness for. Say there is one leap year within those 7 years. So 365 days times 48000 = 17 520 000. Now multiply that by 6 years which is 105 120 000. Now add the leap year total of 17 568 000 to 105 120 000 and you get 122 688 000 in hell for that one sin that's not including what death tacks on for good measure. Now add all other sins you've done though out your lifetime to this figure and get your final total. And no, death will not let your time served be on spiritual time, he is going to let your time served be on earthly time because it was on earth that you committed your sins. So truly good luck to billions of you. Now tell me this, how is your Jesus going to save you when he did not exist and if he did. No he didn't but if he did, tell me how can he over ride death when death is not his kingdom supposedly but Good God's kingdom is? He Jesus cannot override the laws of God – Good God and Allelujah because if he did he would go straight to hell; jail.

A sinner is a sinner. Yes you can change your life for the better but how? Hate has no place with Good God; hence I refuse to spread hate no matter the undertone of some of these books. If there was a better way for me to do this I would but there isn't. Like I told Good God and Allelujah, I refuse to lie for him or anyone. The full truth is what I must give and if you cannot accept the truth then you cannot accept God – Good God and Allelujah.

Good God did not ordain death. We ordained death because we choose death over life and this is wrong. We must choose good and true; clean and positive life over death at all times. Also, we cannot hate based on hue because no one can take hue – hue man skin to Good God. Hence we are told we are changed in the spiritual realm and this is infinitely and indefinitely true.

Hate just get you a place in hell so stop hating. No hate is warranted nor can any of us take hate to God – Good God.

And if you do not comprehend when I say some whites are blacks and some blacks are white. Go to your internet and look up the Ying and the Yang. This picture should be self explanatory. The Blue and White Ying and Yang represents the spiritual realm. Yes like unto the White and Blue Nile. This is life – good and evil; life itself for those who understand over stand and comprehend.

And Sudan forgive me for lashing out like this because you did sign a pact with the devil. The Babylonian and or Arab Empire but I cannot sit and watch someone insight war. You are not his people and as civilized beings we are not to fight. We know the commandments of Good

God and instead of living by his commandments we lie to him and fight, steal, cheat; die. War is not the answer to anything and if we as blacks had stayed true to him Good God and Allelujah we would not find ourselves in the pits of lies, hell and death today. We would not be living in deaths valley, we would be living a life of truth and righteousness. Maybe I care too much. All I know is what this man is doing is wrong. I will not give him right when he is wrong. If you want to help Sudan, truly help the people truthfully. Be there for them in goodness and in truth, but do not spy on them. You are committing a crime but yet the international community condone this wrong. If someone was to set up a spy satellite to spy on America then that country would be looked upon as evil. America would be up in arms and saying that country is a treat to their security and the American People. America would do all to vilify and spread propaganda against that country. And now here you are George Clooney doing the same thing but yet no one is saying anything about it. You are spying on and in another man's land. You are not doing this to help Sudan, you are doing it for your own benefit; their oil. You cannot tell me otherwise because if it was me, I would get all of Africa and their high chiefs together to discuss ways to quell the conflict. Come on now. Both sides, North and South Sudan has elders and chiefs, so why lock them out of your dialog? **_Tell me something. If you are not of the people how the hell are you going to help them?_**

If you know not their history, how are you going to help them?

If you do not speak their language, how are you going to understand them?

How are you going to communicate with them?

You say you are on the side of the South but yet marry someone of the North – someone in the opposite direction? So now tell me, how true are you to South Sudan when you've joined with the North against them? You've just joined death in union hence your triangle is now interlocked and death has you in his hand. *You no longer have the upright triangle of life but the interlocked Star of David – Death. Like I said, you joined death hence if death has not said it, let me. Look up.*

Your sign says – reads, **_WELCOME TO HELL._** *And if you cannot comprehend what I said about joining death. Ask a true Jew that knows the truth. Not an Israeli because they too have joined death hence the interlocking Mogen David. This star is death's star – the union of good and evil. The triangle of life cannot be interlocked with the triangle of death. The triangle of life must infinitely and indefinitely forever ever without end stay separated from the triangle of death.* **_To unify them you are telling Good God and Allelujah that you are not joined and or unified with him, you are joined and or unified with death._**

Now back on track.

Like I said, do to improve you. Change the slum mindset and live. Instead of throwing garbage here there and everywhere. Have a drum and or steel bin to put your garbage in. If there are no garbage trucks in your area design something to burn your garbage in. In designing this something to burn your garbage in, think safety because we do not want the fire to spread and burn your homes down. So truly think and design wisely. Maybe design these burn areas close to water holes but consider the health risks. Seepage into your water holes and or wells.

And know you may not be successful at some things but don't give up trying. Many times we sit and wait for things to happen but it doesn't work that way for many. If sitting and waiting is not working for you, get up and do. That do maybe is to sweep your front and back yard.

It could be taking that trip to the doctor but whatever that something is, make sure you do it and do it for you and your family if you have a family. You matter, so let no one tell you otherwise.

Maybe where you live all zinc surrounds you. Design a zinc house then and make it look pretty. Paint it if you can and decorate the outside. No one has to know you are living in a zinc house if you design it properly and paint it properly.

Make one or two even three bedroom zinc houses – come on now.
Use your mind and think innovatively.

Hey if there are empty barrels and containers around you. Use them for water.
Make wash basins.

Hey if they can make tables and chairs, make tables and chairs with them.
Make beds
Bicycles
Carts to bring your goods to the market.

If there are empty shipping containers around that are abandoned make your home out of these empty abandoned containers. Use your imagination like I've said and design and or paint flowers and or nature on the container to spruce them up. Come on think with me here.

You are important and the surroundings you live in is important. So make your surroundings about you and the good people that you live and or reside with.

No, not all people are good I know this for a fact. But I don't let them get me down. I keep going until I cannot go anymore I take a rest. When I am well rested I go again. That rested period could be for a month or two maybe three. But at the end of the day after my rest period is over I have to go again. I have new life hence the avenues I've failed in I can and do let go. Not always but sometimes. I have to come new because this is new life. So truly learn to listen to good advice and counsel because the life you save at the end of the day is your own.

Remember tomorrow will always come because tomorrow is given. It is us humans that take away our tomorrow.

You can no longer sit on your asses and say God is going to save me; do all for me. He will not save you nor will he do all for you because you are not doing something positive for yourself.

You have to try in order for him to put forth an effort to help you. If you know the water hole is a mile down the road, get up and catch water. He Good God isn't going to get a bucket and catch the water for you.

Yes, when you can't go he will send you help, but you have to put forth the initial effort. This is how he works. And yes sometimes he's slow to help but still don't give up. Remember how many people he has on his plate to help. Not to mention the negative forces and sins that plagues and surrounds earth. So it's not easy for him either. Do for you until he comes along and take charge.

Hey look how many years I've been at this and not one book has been sold to anyone. I buy these books and hand them out free, plus send free copies but I am being ignored.

When I give up and I do give up at times, another avenue comes along and I try that avenue. I even doubt these books and say I am an awful writer because mistakes are in these books.

So as I stay firm and keep trying, I am asking you to do the same until better comes. Like I said, I do get angry and I let my anger get the better of me hence the racism in some of these books. But like I said, not all blacks are blacks and not all whites are whites and the racism is not intentional. You have to know which banner you fall under in order to be saved. Go back to Moses and the blood that was put on the doors of God's people. If I am wrong about the blood forgive me. Hence I tell you to know what banner you fall under because this banner is your saving grace.

Know Good God and Allelujah not just believe in him because belief changes. You have to be solid in him so that when the devil knocks at your door you can rebuke him and banish him to hell.

And it matters not if you think I am the devil. Know that the devil's children had time, 24000 years to change also, but they refused to change. The lies of sin suits them just fine hence they locked themselves in hell indefinitely forever ever. They are going to die because I've told you time and time again, ***GOOD GOD AND ALLELUJAH DOES NOT LOCK ANYONE OUT OF HIS KINGDOM AND OR ABODE. WE ARE THE ONES TO LOCK OURSELVES OUT WITH OUR SINS AND LIES.***

Michelle Jean
September 19, October 1 – 3, 2014
And December 05, 2014

Oh Lord my dream this morning (September 19, 2014).

People; Family, like I said my dream world is getting weird. It seems male death is done with me because he lost and it's female death's turn.

Like I've said, I've been dreaming about kids more and more. Hence as parents we truly have to guard our children and look after them.

Had two vivid dreams but the other one is neither here nor there because it involves another side of my family and I truly do not care what is happening to them. They are not my true family so nothing they do truly concerns me.

Now, I dreamt this lady, black lady and I was telling her my children could see ghosts in the living. I truly don't know why I was telling her this because this dream centered around my last child. After telling her my children could see ghost, I told her I rebuked them (these ghosts) in the name of God. And she said no, I must rebuke them (these ghosts) in the name of Jesus. SHE SAID GOD KILLS. People and Family, my true family I will not even get mad and I did not get mad at her nor did I get mad at Good God and Allelujah. I was told to walk before death and now here this demon - demon black woman in black telling me my beloved, bunnunooonus of a sweet and big up big up Jackfruit and all that is sweet and nice, pure and clean, good and righteous; positive to me kills.

Wow.

Family, I know better hence I truly do better. I know life - the good and true God I truly love, so I can't be bothered with stupid evil spirit's a cum tell mi sey God kill.

Fi har Gad kill but no fimi. Absolutely no one in life can stand up and say life kills. All I have to do is point at nature and the growth in nature. Good grow up and glow.

Good go up and grow up to Good God and Allelujah, so I cannot be bothered with her and her nonsense. Life – good life cannot kill because good and true life is clean and just. Have no time to deal with stupidity of the wicked and evil of the spiritual realm.

Good last from everlasting to everlasting. Good cannot die hence true and good life cannot die. It must continuously grow up forever ever without end. So I am not going to let this fool tell me otherwise. If God killed, he would be dead right now. Not one of us in humanity would be living hence I know the difference between life and death.

Her God is death hence she can come with her lies. As for my children seeing the dead (ghosts), they see certain things in their dreams and they know certain things. Not all but some. Spirituality is something that they don't get into with me in depth. When they can't figure things out they come to me. What they don't know they have these books to read and put things together. Will they read these books?

I hope so because it's their future. I know but I don't know all and all I have are dreams and faces before me but this is my world and not theirs. I have to make sure and ensure that they have a good and true life. In so doing I am not stupid. The talking I do with them have to stop because it seems like they are not listening. This the last of day's kids are stubborn and all they want is their own way. They don't appreciate anything not even nature and this is sad.

I want to escape the concrete jungles of man but they want to stay in it.

I want and need to live and be surrounded by nature, trees and water and they (the younger generation) does not want this.

Why?

It's not like it's going to get easier for them because governments, corporations and people - the citizens of the land made sure they have no future to look forward to.

Our kids have and has become the sacrificial lamb for society - the many.

Dominance and control; death and starvation was always in the cards for wicked and sinful people. But what these wicked and sinful people including governments did not realize is that they wrote their own end literally.

As humans we fail to realize that the life we live in the living determines where we go in the grave. Billions are slated for hell hence life will go on and you are going to die.

Michelle Jean
September 19, 2014

Postscript

To this woman who told me God kills, I am going into the world you know. Take note because I dedicate Smokie Norful "I KNOW TOO MUCH ABOUT HIM" to you.

Listen to him when he said, "you can't tell me nothing, cause I know God. I know God for myself. He's been with me when I didn't know how I would make it. God you were there Lord."

Truly take the song in because "there is nothing you can say or do to destroy my piece of mind." There is nothing you can do for me not to trust him.

You cannot destroy my true love of him. Satan couldn't and you definitely cannot. Know this, I've been through the ringers of hell and the devil failed; could not rock me so what say you? Yes you can speak and I hear you because you are heard, but when it comes to my true love of Good God and Allelujah you cannot rock me because he has all my trust and truth. I know the God of Life – good and true life; so please do not try nor come around me anymore because I will make you sorry. Know and truly tell your counterparts this for me. Good God and Allelujah is my truth and protector that I more than truly love unconditionally. God isn't dead nor does he kill. Despite what the song said that God died to set him free. God isn't dead and can never be dead and humanity lives. We would all be dead with him. If he God – Good God and Allelujah died all of humanity including hell and death; this earth and universe would die along with him, so truly do not try anything.

Yes at times I doubt him and I tell him of my doubts.

I blast him and get angry at him but with death I cannot do this. Death isn't concerned about anyone hence I choose life, because life does listen despite what I say and write at times.

I know the difference in time and the vibrations of time in time hence reaching him (Good God and Allelujah) is difficult. So clear off and don't come back to my door. I truly don't need you nor do I need to hear you. Hence listen to "I UNDERSTAND" by Smokie Norful because I more than understand and over stand. You don't understand nor will you comprehend me and Good God and Allelujah. Hence I dedicate this song (I UNDERSTAND) to me and all who are going through the struggle like me. No matter my lonely thoughts, days and world, I will continue to hold unto him. Good God and Allelujah is my winner and he deserves all that is good and true from me and his family. Hence no weapons formed against me and his children and people shall prosper. Fred Hammond. I truly love him more than unconditionally and I refuse to let you rock me and take him from me because Good God is my right and I will always choose true life over death infinitely and indefinitely forever ever unconditionally without end.

Michelle

Darkness flows
Night fall
Clouds
The moon

Full and radiant
Beautiful
Serene

I see life all around
The beauty of nature
All green

I notice the heavens - sky
No stars can be found

Concrete jungles, electrical lights all around

All that the eye can see you see. Fluorescent lights is all you see. Fluorescent lights all around.

Nothing natural anymore

Natural humans can hardly be found. All there is is vanity.
Vain people everywhere in search of what others call beauty.
Vain people that hate self and cannot see the beauty in self.

Oh man if some of them could truly take a look in the mirror and see self; see that all they bought for self is truly ugly. (Cosmetic surgery).

Truly does anyone want to be with them?
All that money paid just for me to run and hide.
Money wasted; not well spent.

Damn boy, girl you paid all that money to look like a clown.
No one can be a human Barbie
Ken

Get real and get a life
Truly love you because in truth I am tired of seeing fake ass beauty.

You're a prop that is broken down
You're my oh damn - it's a frown.

You're a court gesture
Corporate bought
Yes you're sold on the stock market hence the cosmetic industry.

You were played
Had because the doctors have your hard earned money.

You played the game
Lost your life to greed - fame
But all's good for all who know

Yes life is different
Looked at differently

For me life is precious
The pure spirit (energy) within; true and natural beauty.

Life is energy
All affects life including the moon.

Yes the moon is out
It's full - pretty
Serene
Bright
Night light
Your heavenly charm; beauty.

Michelle Jean
September 08, 2014

Dear God what is live without serenity?

What is life without true peace?
Hope
True love

We are but energy beings that have lost our way.
We know things but truly do not know.

Life isn't a game, it's real.

We are surrounded by nature - green foliage.
Life's energy

Life is sweet no matter our struggles, turmoil; pain.

We can't give up because nature is there to warm our hearts – soul.
Nature doesn't give up so why should we?

Nature is there to take us back home
There to ease our minds
Soften our heavy load.
Cleanse our soul.

Nature is calm
Nature soothes you
Relaxes the mind
Calms your spiritual being
World.

Michelle Jean
September 08, 2014

There is so much that I want and need to say and do. But it seems there's a communication problem between me and you.

Yes distance come into play but why should it though?

Our long distance relationship can work. So why am I the one doing all the talking and writing?

Why am I doing all the calling?

You know my name and number Good God so call me like I call you.

Ah man there's something wrong.

Good God are you truly gone?

No you're not truly gone. It seems like you've become lazy.

No not lazy but yet lazy. No I have no other word to describe our communication troubles - problems. So I am going to leave things at lazy.

Michelle Jean
September 08, 2014

I don't want to be funny nor do I want to look at the funnies today.

I need to be in your arms resting if not sleeping.

Yes I am lazy
Want to be pampered by you
Yes everybody.

Yes I am bored
Weather has changed.

No life just autumn
Then winter, oh hum

Seychelles here comes Michelle
Swaziland too; maybe

Yes this is me on my overly boring days

Mood swings, mood swings
No heat

Summer is done hence life has become boring – dreary, dull; dead.
Well not dead, life is just hibernating again.

Daylight is going, only night light, fall. Oh man if only I can or could jump from one country
to the next to avoid night fall.

Yes I need something
Need to fly away to be me.

Yes I want to fly away and come back another day.

Want to be in my own little world away from modern day society – civilization.

Yes I want to be busy but busy how?

Who knows and who cares. Autumn and winter is so damned depressing; near.

Too damned cold hence this is the reality of my boring world.
Day.

Michelle Jean
September 14, 2014

I'm bored, I'm bored
What a dull life
Day

Yes I'm bored.
Bored, bored, bored

So because I am bored, I am going to annoy you; bore you too.

Want to lay naked writing
Want to walk naked on the beach. Well my beach that is.

Yes this is my own private property.
World

Want to go crazy making love. Need to release my tension that is building up.

Shit damn wow. I so don't want to go home.

Do I need mental rescuing?

No. I just hate autumn and winter. Give me spring and summer all day long. Hence I yearn for the warmth of the sun.

Well maybe a man.

Yes I yearn to enjoy all that is cool and nice; warm and fun.
Ah the beach and hotel life.

Michelle Jean
September 14, 2014

Ah what the hell
It's nightfall and it's getting dark

Getting to hate this ho hum and boring life.

Want to fly the coop and settle somewhere
Somewhere truly calm and nice; warm

Yes I want to leave the devil's world
Want to leave the prison walls of my own God.
Apartment

Caged, caged, caged. I feel caged.
What's the point of me truly loving him when I can't have freedom and be free my own way?

What's the point of truly loving him when I can't vacation with him?
What's the point if I can't truly hold his hand?
What's the point if I feel so all alone?

Yes I am going to go insane. Hence I need my own little island where I can do my own damned thing without him. But then again, I do understand, comprehend because he too needs time to make our world perfect for me and him. So yes I truly understand and over stand.

Michelle Jean
September 14, 2014

I so can't take the stress anymore. My chest is hurting me more and more.

Can't take the morning stress of waking up my kids especially my last one; son.

To be honest with the way he's going, I truly do not see him with a future; nor do I see him graduating high school and this is pretty sad.

I truly can't fight with him anymore for his own good. Hence I give up. Totally give up on him when it comes to his education and future.

The school year has just begun and already he's missing and skipping school.

With my chest hurting me more and more it's a matter of time before I have a heart attack. I truly can't take the heartache and pain; stress anymore. He's putting me through too much and I've reached my breaking point again.

You want better for your children and you try to do all for them so that they can succeed and have a better future, but they are failing you. They choose the wrong road and or path to follow.

You sacrifice so much for them and they don't appreciate you. They don't try to achieve. I truly can't comprehend these black; young black and stupid kids of today. And to be honest with you from what I see, they are the ones messing up their future not me and or you. They cause their parents so much undue stress and heartache like mine to the point where you want to leave them and run. Run so far that they can't find you just like you Good God. Come on now. We don't listen; hence you are gone from billions of us. Now we are playing catch up, trying to find you.

No wonder so many black moms are dropping down. It's because of these stupid kiss-mi-ass kids that refuse to listen. Like I've said, you do all and or try to do all for them so that they can have a better future but they refuse to listen. They want things the hard and difficult way whilst putting undo pressure and stress on you the parent.

I am sick and I'm sacrificing all including my health for them and instead of easing the stress and pressure on me by waking up and going to school they can't do that. You constantly have to be waking up. You are constantly yelling and screaming being stressed out amongst other things. Nothing is working and I'm fed up.

I refuse to go through this another year with my last one and daughter.

No man, I am fed up of the crap I am living in hence shortly I am gone. I can't take the stress anymore and I so have to put myself first.

I have to think of me and my health, sanity and recovery. If I am trying, doing all that is good and true for you; help yourself and go to school.

Some things I cannot do but if I am trying to help you just get up and go to school. Get your education because education is vital to all. If you can't read and write you are going to be left behind. If you can't read the financial pages then you are screwed. Come on now.

Don't stress me out
Do your homework
Get up in the mornings; have breakfast and leave out on time to go to school.

Don't yell at me and tell me to leave if I ask you if you want cereal or tea. I'm trying to help you but yet you are disrespecting me.

So what the hell is the point? I do your chores when I can so you don't have to do them. So do all that is good to help you but even that you can't do. So where the hell am I going wrong? Your future - good tomorrow is important to me, but if you don't want a good tomorrow then how am I going to help you?

As a mother my job is to ensure that things are right and okay with you, but if you and your wicked and evil will is destroying me, how the hell can I help you?

How can I be of any good to you?

Make it easy for me so that you have me around when things get a little rough and tough - stressed. As a mother I tell you (my children), if you work save your money, I don't need the rent. If you can help with the bills help but do for you, save and get ahead. I will take the blunt of the force and hardship so that you can be secured in life - your tomorrow. I'm getting older, you are just coming; but noooo you are not listening, nor do you comprehend my true love for all of you. With me doing all I am doing for you, help me also out of the goodness of your heart. Even though I do not charge you rent some months contribute to the rent. Help pay the rent so I too can get ahead and be debt free and or stress free. I need better for all my children but I can't sit and talk anymore. If you don't want better for self that's fine, but don't look at me for help later on because I will be gone. My oldest ones, at least my oldest one he's listening and it's him that I must make a good and better future for. For the other ones, if they can't listen then shall surely feel.

Hopefully one day I will get truly healthy and do all I need to do for him and him alone. He listens to good and true council and at times he falls off the wagon but he's trying. The other ones can blow because they like things the hard way and all they are to me is just plain and all out stress most of the time.

Michelle Jean
September 15, 2014

As parents some of you know the stress and pain I am talking about. Things are not going to get easier for our children tomorrow because the harvest comes.

Food will be scarce for some.
Lakes and rivers are going to dry up.

Water at least that which is left of it will become undrinkable hence many lands are going to become barren, lay in ruin; waste.

Many are going to be homeless.

As a parent you are trying but your children are failing you. Yes sometimes we fail self but in many cases our children fail us with the bad choices they make.

As a parent I do my best to encourage my children so that they can and will succeed. I have my dream and dreams and I am fulfilling them (my dreams). All I want and need is for my children to accomplish something. Not for me but for them and their future, their future children; family. I've lived my life and still living it. I cannot go back in time and change anything because I've lived that time already. All I can do is move forward and continue on in life until my spirit cannot take anymore it flees the flesh; the confines of its prison.

I don't know, but is this too much to ask of my children when it comes to making good and wise choices so that they excel in life?

Live your life good and clean and do all for the good of you and for you.

If I am making a positive headway for you, take it and help you. Help the ones that are helping you in a positive and good way. Don't be like our ancestors of old and today that don't want good and better for self.

Listen, I've struggled with my kids. Good God and Allelujah have and has struggled with his kids (children); me and you. I am learning to listen and do good so why can't you; our kids?

I see the future, feel and know certain things and if you are getting life the easy way take it and live. Build you and your life in a positive and good as well as clean way.

Why take the hard road if you don't have to?

People, Fam; I truly don't know hence I know how Good God feels when it comes to raising ungrateful and stiff necked kids - children. As parents you have to be constantly drilling things in these kids head and I am tired of it.

If you know you go to a school that wears uniform, wear your uniform and or uniform shirt. Don't leave home without it. I shouldn't have to tell you this day in and day out but yet I have to constantly tell you this virtually each and every day. Why?

Soon and very soon when Mama is gone don't cry because I am not coming back. I am going to live my life and enjoy it to the fullest without you and the bullshit you put me through. Yes I know my end but when is the issue?

Trust me I am learning hence my escape is coming soon and this time around I don't care if I end up in the streets.

Fed up am I of the constant talking.
The headaches and lack of respect for my home and surroundings including me.

I'm tired of the bullshit that some of you are doing hence bringing shame and disgrace to my family. You know what, I am still facing the storm and the flowers I've given Good God is drooping, withering. I cannot save them nor can he Good God and it's a crying shame. I guess what we are expecting from God - Good God he cannot deliver. His deliverance is so not physical and or of my world but of his.

Not even my true love and joy could save our flowers so what is the point in any of this?

What is the point of giving someone something that is going to die? Maybe this is what he's trying to tell me and show me. Maybe he's trying to show me my end.

Maybe he's trying to tell me when you give flowers give them with roots so that they can live not wither and die. I guess this is the message he wanted me to know in some way amongst other things.

Yes it's hurtful because in many ways like I've said, I was expecting him to save these flowers and not make them wither and die. It's weird because you hear people talk about how God has rescued them, but yet I am forgetting their God is not my God. My God can only protect and nothing else I guess.

With him at times I feel imprisoned; as if I am in prison looked away by walls - prison walls and this is scary.

Depressed I am but not with me in a sense but with the happenings of life. Depressed about seeing death all the time; our death in time. But with all these deaths, I get no solution and or solutions to give to man - humanity to save self. I got to save my homeland Jamaica but not humanity on a whole.

We say go to church, but I cannot go into the whore houses of death. Churches are a physical prison just as hell is a spiritual prison. I guess as humans we cannot comprehend the scope of our spiritual church. I know for a fact that there is a spiritual church and I've not touched on this church because I truly do not comprehend her.

I see her and she is all powerful, but what does she have to do with me because I am running from her and refuse to make a connection with her in all of this. Not because of fear but because of lack of comprehension; knowledge. I truly do not know what her church represent because in her church there are no crosses of death just another form of life I guess.

No singing. There is but a delay in time because they are always late. Things that I know already, they are telling me and this is weird. I guess they are my confirmations that I am true. They are the ones to confirm the truth; weird.

I know about the Crystal City and she who resides outside of this city. She protects this city and she is black. All the females of sight and wisdom are black. Except for that one white woman. Chinese are black and they are a part of the city and life of truth this I know. Hence prosperity comes through them (the Chinese) in the spiritual world of giving.

Like I said; many things I know but this great resistance by me in regards to her is confusing because I truly do not know where I fit in with her and what she wants with me and or of me.

I know Father God but Mother God is being resisted by me because of the church that is associated with her in the spiritual realm. I truly don't like churches people and with her coming to me with her church is driving me crazy because I have no control of my spirit. In the spiritual world my spirit is weak. I call it weak because it can be controlled by a higher force and this is sad.

Maybe it's me hence I truly have to find me. I have to find where I belong with me and me alone. I know where I belong in the universe but when it comes to me and me, I truly do not know where I belong.

God is not a factor because in a lot of sense I am trying to get rid of him and live my life for me good and clean. I can no longer live for him because he's not living for me.

He's there but he rarely speaks and I truly need someone that can speak to me, teach me how to heal me and deliver me from me and the problems that surround me.

Am I broken?

Yes because I am in a place where I truly don't want to be and when I seek escape, I can't escape. Like I said, it feels like I am in a prison. It's as if I am caged and there is no escape for me. I want and need to do so much but yet can't. I am restricted in doing so. And I refuse to hang around a God that restricts me from doing all the good that I need to do.

My greatest desire is to give to others so that they can better their lives, self and I cannot do this. I am imprisoned - limited. It seems like success is not for me and if I want success, I have to sell my soul and I refuse to sell my soul to the devil and or anyone.
Life is worth living but the restrictions of life are not for me or anyone.

Yes this is sad but its life I guess. You want so much good for life and life's people, but yet Life is restricting you in all that you want and need to do and this is sad. Yes I know nothing happens before its time but what about me and what I need in my time?

So shortly I have to do me hence I so want to disobey more and more. Yes I know this is due to the depressive nature of the changing seasons. I can't help it but if I could I would.
Escape is there for me but the cost, vacation packages are so damned expensive. All is based

on double occupancy and not single occupancy.

Even train tickets are expensive. All is done so that you can't escape the prison walls of these damned concrete and ugly jungles of man and his sickening designs.

Man has and have made things so expensive that you cannot travel on your own to other lands. Then they complain and say they don't have enough and or making enough money. Shit stop making things so damned expensive. You want people to travel, make things affordable for the average person that can't afford your 900$ plus for a room. I want to travel but I so don't want to share a room with anyone. I want to be alone and vegetate for a week or two, so cater to us the can't afford your expensive package people. Why can't we get flight and hotel; all inclusive packages to Cuba, St. Lucia, Costa Rico, Antigua, St. Vincent, Tobago for 850$ or even 750$ come on now?

Yes make it all inclusive because some of us like me are stressed out and miserable. All we want is to go someplace and unwind for a week or two. I do. I want to rest and unwind but like everything else in this world. Nothing is done to accommodate the poorer class that can't afford your high end air fares and hotel. Hence many of us are prisoners in cities, towns and countries we truly do not want to be in.

It's autumn and winter will soon be here. I can't take the winter but I am stuck, stuck in a city that I truly want to escape forever ever indefinitely from.

Damn going to BC is a damned chore.

Train tickets are worse than plane fares. So how the hell can we talk about tourism when all the prices you are given is definitely out of reach for the poor like me?

Hence God is not on my table of wanting to continue with anymore. It's just too damned hard trying to obey him when it comes to vacations. So I am going to have to go another route.

Michelle Jean
September 15th and 21st 2014

I am waiting hence I have to answer my own call.

Have to be there for me
Have to help me
Have to listen to me

Life isn't easy when it comes to your achievements, finances; goals.

There are days when I do give up like now. For some strange reason as soon as Labour Day comes and it gets cold, depression comes. Less daylight and too much nightlight. It's as if the strength of the sun is gone; weakened by the cold - ice of the moon. It's as if your world is ending; has become affected; sick.

It's as if the spirit is broken
Tired
Can't go anymore
Move

So the mood swings and changes come
Your heart and spirit feels down
Flawed
Broken

Ah what a life when you cannot truly grow; glow.

Yes I need the sun - heat of the sun to warm my body; keep my cells alive, active and firm. I need the sun to keep my spirit from going insane.

Need the sun in my world of loneliness; depression.
Boredom

Now the withering stage begins hence the call of my body.

Ah summer is gone
The heat is gone
Body function going; have limited balance.

Ah my body is failing
I feel like I am an alcoholic walking. Feet are not firmly on the ground.

Wobble, Wobble
I am the walking bobble head doll on any given day.

Body drunk and I'm not even an alcoholic.

If you were to see me you would think I am drunk out of my mind, but yet you cannot find a tat or a drop of alcohol in me; my body.

Ah well welcome to my world hence I am limited in what I can do.
I am caged
Feel caged
Yes more health woes because of the cold.

Damn I need extra clothing
Layers
God forbid.
Yes I dare but don't; won't.

Hell no not Russia in the cold.

Yes many will take offence to my use of alcoholic but the wobbly wobblies you will not understand, comprehend. So I had to use alcoholic because this lifestyle best suit's the condition I am in now that it's getting cold.

I have to say in my home.

Do not dare venture into the cold without proper layers – clothing and even that don't help.

Ah well, got to go with the flow when summer comes again to deliver his and her warmth even if it is just briefly; a limited stay.

Yes it would be nice to go away for an extended period of time like 6 months out of each year but the finances is truly not there.

I have to take things as they are and bare with the intolerable cold.

Michelle Jean
September 15th and 21st, 2014

It's weird how life is
How man's quest for dominance and control have led to the destruction of his own.

As I see the world today, I see the lies that has been told in the name of science
The superior and inferior race
The God defect
Religious control

As humans we think we are intellectual beings but we are savages living a savages dream.

We are savages that kill
Eat and consume each other

Savages that have been living in death's trap for thousands of years, billions for some.

Savages that think they know better but truly do not know
Truly don't know better nor can do better

In all I know, we humans wonder if there are intelligent life out there.

Yes this is a question that has plagued man - humanity until this day. But how dumb can we be in asking this question.

There are intelligent life, forces and people for the lack of a better word out there. The fact is, they don't want to have anything to do with us because we are savages; uncivilized and uncultured. We kill, kill each other and hate each other. We kill to eat, eat each other and drink each other.

We are not intelligent because we as humans cannot share the earth with Life, the trees and animals of the earth.

We are murderers, killers that kill and destroy everything for our lesser gain and not for greater gain; better good – positive.

We humans are the inferior beings because we know not the art and truth for good and better living.

We are greedy beings that destroy hence superior races - beings wants nothing to do with us.

They run and hide from us.
They can't be found because they don't want to become polluted like us and by us.
We are the unclean ones and they are the clean; the clean ones.
They are life; know life and we are the dead ones – the walking dead.

We are disease carriers that lack intellect; intelligence. Hence every so often (24 000 years) we die on a massive scale. We die, are eliminated because we don't know how to live.

We truly don't care.

We die because we are sinful. We do not know how to listen and stop our sinful and deceitful ways.

We do not know how to live; truly can't live clean.

We go around and around debating life, even say we come from monkeys – animals. Hence we cannot comprehend and know life.

How can humans come from monkeys?

What an idiotic thought and view but yet we say we are intelligent, civilized; cultured.

How can a civilized man – humans come from an animal?

So what we are saying then is that animals, the monkey is smarter than man?
Monkeys and animals are our parents?

But then I shouldn't dispute this because animals don't make weapons of mass destruction to destroy and kill each other.

Animals don't design and create diseases to kill each other; other animals.

Animals don't build concrete jungles and kill the environment they live in.

Animals don't pollute the waterways with poison; herbicides, pesticides; chemicals.

Hence yes animals are smarter than man because they know how to live and respect the land they are living in.

They live with nature and they know nature. Hence they respect nature; their environment.

As humans we are pathetic and ridiculous hence we've become pathetic and ridiculous; uncivilized and illiterate. To think we put ourselves in high esteem; but yet are so dumb to believe and trust crap such as evolution. Hence humanity knows not where they are coming from nor do they know where they are going.

No wonder God eludes us because of the crap we believe in.

The brain is a tidal wave of knowledge that flows up not down. But with all that said, humanity lives down (death) not up (life).

Knowledge, the knowledge of the universe is in man, it's man that forgot the key; combination to unlock this door. Hence time is the master lock to death and not life. Life cannot be locked away because the door to life is always open. We are the ones to close the doorway of life and throw away the key.

Once the key is gone you cannot retrieve it, so truly good luck in life because death surely comes – has your number and combination; key.

Evil kills hence man is evil.
Man kill and wonder why they die.

We all know the wages of sin is death but we follow death anyway. But yet with all this said, we say we are civilized, educated, wise; intelligent.

Wow

The way we deceive ourselves into thinking we are smart and intelligent.

If we were so smart, we would know the opening to life and not close our doors to life and die.

If we were so smart, intelligent and civilized, how come man - humanity is slated to die globally shortly before 2032?

If man we were so smart, how come we are destroying life, hence soon to be extinct in the flesh globally real soon?

If man we were so smart, how come we cannot preserve life and walk away from death?

We live for death hence we create and or design weapons for death to die?

Why design and create diseases that kill people and lands – die?

Why deplete the resources of the earth if we know these resources are important to our existence?

We say we have it all, but truly do not know that Earth is dying and we are dying with her.

W say we have it all and know it all, but yet do not know it all nor do we have it all.

We kill all in her (earth) and kill ourselves, but yet say we are intelligent, wise and civilized; superior and intelligent beings.

We take life from her (Earth) without knowing that we are taking life from our self. Hence humans are not intelligent. We are stupid beings that live to kill and destroy; die. We've paved the way for our own destruction, hence we are on a planet all to our selves; own.

This is our physical hell. Hence death comes to take the spirit from the flesh so we can die a more painful and harsher death in the spiritual realm.

Like I've said in one of my other books, we do not think of our spirit. We do not see our spirit as life but our spirit is life. It is the spirit that keeps the flesh alive for a time. Ones the time of flesh has expired, it (your spirit) moves on to another level. This level is determined by you the individual on earth. Meaning if you live an evil life, you will know your sentence in the grave. This is your judgment and no one can override your sentence not even your god and gods because your triangle is turned down.

You created your own hell with the sins and or evils you did and or do on earth.

If you are good you cannot be judged because your good outweighs your sins.

And no, Jesus cannot petition Good God and Allelujah for you the sinner. The law clearly states, _**"THE WAGES OF SIN IS DEATH,"**_ so if you sin and have not made amends for your sins here on earth, you are going to die. The law is set and it is also set in time. Meaning that this law is not only physical but it is infinitely and indefinitely spiritual. I've told you, the life you live in the living determines where you go in the afterlife; meaning when the spirit sheds its prison – the flesh and or body.

Michelle Jean
September 15, 2014

It's weird how we kill each other, do all to die.

Weird how we can't see our own destruction; extinction.

It's amazing how we pollute and destroy everything whilst thinking we still have a future.

How dumb are we to thing this; so?
How dumb are we that we cannot see that we've destroyed ourselves?

We've depleted the resources of earth and nothing is balanced; it's all unbalanced.

We talk about the eco system of earth and I have to ask, what eco system? Have we not destroyed the coral reefs, glaciers - ice lands all in the advancement of greed and political gain – man?

Have we not set the course for our own destruction and now we are going to be destroyed real soon?

Panic, panic, yes panic. I'm hitting the panic button because the extinction of man – humanity; wicked and evil people is before 2032.

Yes time is winding down and many lands are already doomed.

We played sin's game - the game of death and lost. We forgot that sin was only for a time then death fully comes and all will be lost – gone. Death must take his or her own.

We did not learn from the past, but yet we say we have great IQ's. Have Masters and PhD's. Yet in all we say we have, we have nothing because man is slated to die real soon.

In all we say we have, we have death hence we are going to die.

In all we did, we could not stop our own deaths; extinction, our own destruction.

We say we are humans, but yet know not the true HUE OF MAN, what makes us HUE MAN (human). Crazy yes. Hence man has turned hue, the hue of man into something vile and disgusting; hated and condemned.

Michelle Jean
September 15, 2014

It's September 21, 2014 and I don't want to write and think anymore. All I want is to be in my own little world away from all that we say is hue man (human).

We know not self hence we hate others; hate self.

We say we are civilized but yet do not know that civilized beings do not want anything to do with us. We hate, kill and destroy; hence they flee from destruction; all that is negative and evil.

Civilized hue mans (humans) do not create strife and hate.

They do not kill; but work in unison with all that is in the universe including earth. But now earth is excluded because of the nastiness we as humans do on land – in earth.

Civility is not with man hence God is not with man. All that we are not to do, we do hence becoming the disobedient ones; the condemned and dead ones.

We are the ones that refuse to listen. So because of this, we are going to be extinct real soon.

It's 2014 and each year we get closer to our own destruction; extinction. As humans we cannot blame anyone but self because we live for greed and do all for greed – sin.

We do not think of the consequences, hence we cannot learn; know not the truth in all that we do.

So as I close this book, I close in truth and await what is to come for me and you real soon.

Yes I have life and I have to live it to the best of my ability given the little resources that I have; the circumstances I live in.

Michelle Jean
September 21, 2014

And if you are evil, please do not latch on to me because I refuse save you. Many of you hurt people; hence I have to do that which is right and true for all the people you willingly and knowingly hurt.

I so do not want anyone of you that is wicked and evil to latch on to me.

I have to find the house and or build the mansion of God – Good God and Allelujah. Once this is done, I am so gone. Well I need to be and not think of what is going to happen to you. Yes its Noah's time all over again hence truly good luck to man – humanity; billions of you because billions will not be saved literally. This is not a scare tactic, this is mans reality globally real soon. Yes many have said the end of time was in 2012 or whatever, but it could not be because the devil – Satan as you call him did not transfer his power to anyone until 2013. I've told you in another book the lands that were expecting this power. The Harlot (England) as told in revelations did not get this power. A woman did not get this power but a black man did; hence he must take the seat of the harlot and govern. He must also unseat the President of The United States Barak Obama because he Barak failed to secure the faith of his people – the Amers – Americans; the Southern lands.

If you are under the protection of Good God and Allelujah I cannot neglect you. I have to receive you but you have to be truthful to you; self; him and her.

You have to want and need better for self; you.

Yes the doors will be open soon and when they do we will be happy together. The mood swings are here, but this is because of the change in weather. The lack of sunlight in the dead months - the autumn and winter months.

Summer comes again and like you I have to wait until it gets here for me to live again.

Pain comes now for the wicked glory to God because all who hurt willingly and knowingly must pay. Evil's time has come and truly woe be unto man – billions. ***<u>Woe be unto the Jews that call themselves Jews and are of the Synagogue of Satan. Just as there are real – true Jews, there are Babylonian Jew and truly woe be unto them (every Babylonian Jew) because they the Babylonian Jews have and has deceived man – humanity.</u>*** *So because of this none can be found under the order of God. None will be shielded from the harvest because of lies and deceit. All their names are taken from the Book of Life and put in the Book of the Dead; meaning they are hell bound, hell is their new home. Not one offspring will find favour with Good God and Allelujah infinitely and indefinitely for more than infinite and indefinite lifetimes and generations to come without end. Their ancestor's names are also taken out of the Book of Life and put in the Book of the Dead indefinitely forever ever without end. All the wickedness of the Jews – Babylonian Jews have and has been declared condemned hence they are judged and found guilty of more than crimes against humanity in the physical and spiritual realm. **<u>They've been found guilty of crimes against Good God and his people and for this; there is no remittance of sin. None is given unto them.</u>*** No merit hath they because they steal the history and heritage of the children of Good God and Allelujah and tainted it for their own prophets (profits) greedy and evil means; gain. Thus saith the Lord thy God meaning it is so. And no, no one look to me for a saving grace for them because He Good God and Allelujah know that I will give them none if I am the saving grace of man – humanity. He Good God and Allelujah including his true people have my word on this for all eternity and for more than infinite and indefinite lifetimes and generations to come indefinitely. I too lock them out hence my back is turn to them in truth – goodness and truth of Good God and Allelujah. They lied; told lies on Good God and Allelujah and I'm to override this? Never and neither will Good God. You don't lie on someone like this come on now man. You lied on Good God and now look at the world today. Riddled with sin; death. How are you the chosen ones when the God of Life you lie on; tell lies on?

Know that a Jew – true Jew is not governed by the evil and wicked laws of men. They are governed by truth – true love, honesty, true peace; the truth of Good God. They are just hence they live just without violence and strife; hate.

In the kingdom of Good God and Allelujah there is no hate.

There is no strife and lies.

There is no violence and wars; diseases.

No superiority of flesh because God – Good God is not flesh but spirit – true life and energy.

There are no hues like in the hue of man. Hence man cannot see the life of many in the dark.

There is life in the dark but if you do not have the eye to see (sight), you cannot see. Hence humanity has and have lost their sight of truth; goodness and truth; good and true life.

So because of this Good God and Allelujah cannot save billions because billions do not know him nor do they belong to him. Hence the different gods' humanity praise and worship; serve here on earth.

Michelle Jean
September 21 and October 08, 2014
And December 05, 2014

It's September 22nd 2014 and my night have been horrible. No wonder I am stressed. I have stress in the physical and stress in the spiritual realm. I am stressed out all around.

Stressed by my children and school and stressed by the demons of hell in the spiritual world.

I am about to crack because I truly need to get rid of the spiritual troubles - woes in my life and nights. It feels like God - Good God don't exist to me anymore because evil continuously find me and I am fed up.

I guess this is for my own good because I wanted to thread in dirty waters and I truly know better. So because I know better I have to do better for the better good and not the better evil - my curiosity and or sexual needs.

Some things I know. I also know what they mean but my dreams are becoming more confusing like I've said. Hence my physical world is stressed to the max at times. And in all honesty, I want and need to be normal hence I so have to walk away from the dream world.

Need to walk away from my sight because I feel as if I am all alone and no one can comprehend what I see and know; what I am going through. I need to live dirty so that God and these spirits can't bother me anymore. And the way for me to do this is to do all that is forbidden and unclean to me and walk in the dirty and unclean world of humanity.

My world is not easy, hence I have too much stress and pain in both worlds and I am fed up of it all. My goodness and sanity is another issue because as soon as I want to do something that does not conform to the goodness and better good of the spirit world, I am being reminded of it and being taunted - set up. All the good I want and need to do cannot come to me and if it does come to me, it takes years and this is so not fair in my book and so not fair to me. But I have to contend with it. But no more because I am not the scapegoat or goat for the spiritual wicked. And no matter how much I complain, God cannot see this. Hence I've got to walk away from it all but can't. This is my destiny, my calling and no matter the pain I feel, I must endure.

I can't let him (Good God) feel pain - my pain and hurt; torment. I know my life is not fair when it comes to certain things so why the hell should I continue to feel pain?

Yes I am angry. Why should I put up with spiritual bullshit?

It's too much on me. Hence I am broken mentally, physically and spiritually. And yes I know how Solomon felt when he freaking went mad. Even when you are trying to walk on the road of righteousness and truth; cleanliness, you still have obstacles and this should not be. You should be able to walk this road (the road of truth) stress free and truthfully. Come on now. But yet I forget at times that I am living in the valley of Death with his and her wicked and evil people including governments.

Yes the road of righteousness is a hard road to walk on and I refuse to walk on this hard road anymore. I truly can't do this by myself hence I need good true and positive help all the time.

Will I come off the road of truth?

No, but on the days when I am overcome with problems I write like this. The road of truth is mine hence no matter how I say I am coming off this road I cannot. I guess in many ways when things are not going my way, I have to write like this because this is my venting process and you are my listeners. Writing like this keep me strong and grounded. Hence I still have hope all around for a better tomorrow.

So hopefully soon you can take my hand and we can walk hand in hand together.

Do I need this for me and you?

Yes I do in truth.

Like I said, it's hard for me and when you are going it alone it's doubly hard if not three times as hard and this is so not good.

Just this morning I dreamt my sister. We were in an opening - a open field of green - green grass. The place looks like the field or opening of where I live. She was telling me she went to her friend's house and they had lots of food. She couldn't take any of the food to carry for me. Something to this effect because I wasn't truly penetrating the dream. All I was penetrating was the thin slice of jackfruit. She could not take any of the food for me like I said, so she took a piece of jackfruit for me. The jackfruit was a thin slice like I said. It was skinny and I noticed how skinny the jackfruit is and it did not look fully ripe to me. This wasn't a regular fat jackfruit because you know how fat jackfruits can be. She went on to tell me how her children were complaining. I can't remember if the complaint was because she was giving me the jackfruit but she did say they were complaining.

I guess she didn't listen to the complaints of her children because she cut the jackfruit in half for me and her and you could see the yellow of the jackfruit and how beautiful and shinny it was. Before she cut the jackfruit it wasn't that yellow but when she cut it to share the jackfruit with me it was a beautiful yellow. So I truly don't know that this means.

I also dreamt I went to her house. I don't know what I was looking for but I went into the kitchen and there was a roast pig that was partially eaten in her kitchen close to the sink and or in the sink. I cannot remember if the small roasted pig was in the sink but the partially eaten small roasted pig was in her kitchen. I left out the kitchen and saw her husband. He had a red and black lumber jacket on with black pants. He looked proper - official in his attire. I can't remember if I asked him if he was going out and if he told me he was coming back from a meeting. But he was dressed to impress in the colours. He looked done up and proper like a professional business man. What I find weird about this dream is, is the fact that he was driving me somewhere. I think it was a trip. So maybe he and my sister and or his family is going to go on a trip real soon. Probably in 2015.

I know what the colours mean - represent hence I am going to leave well enough alone and watch this dream. Pigs are not clean people hence I have to tell my sister to guard her health because something is so not right in her home. Have to tell her to talk to her oldest daughter because she is going away soon.

The day before this one, I dreamt about going down a river on a raft - logs and there was green trees around. A forest all around. The place was beautiful because it was like islands in the sea and or ocean – water.

I know they say green is disappointment but oh well. I guess disappointment is all around me but who the hell cares at this point. I know the tragedy of my life in regards to the spiritual world wanting me to fail – die.

I don't know why but I keep dreaming about this black woman and her church in the spiritual realm. She is stuck in my head and I cannot share her hence I went on the computer to look up Pagan Symbolism and find the descriptions of these symbols weird - a joke. Have we come so far in life that we have to believe in symbolic lies?

We know not what these symbols mean because humanity knows not how they came into being. To us well you, humanity began with Adam and Eve and this is wrong. Humans existed long before Adam and Eve; hence we truly do not know about the hues of man and or men hence humans and or human. Our hue (flesh) represents Life and Death, the White and Blue Nile. Nor do we know the powers of the mind because we limit ourselves in life and this is wrong. What we think life is is not what life is.

Death cannot change, it must remain dead. But life changes, meaning life grow up to Good God and a better world and this is what we as humans do not know; cannot attain in our polluted and or unclean world and state of mind.

Our skin fail but our spirit cannot fail. It (our spirit) is governed by a different energy and hue. A different kind of hue man; human energy.

As humans we do not know how our life and or lives began, hence we believe in a lot of crap; the negative because this is all we see and know. This is one of the reasons why death comes; we die and this is sad. We die because of our sins; lies and this is true for the physical and spiritual world.

I guess we cannot come to the realization that all we know is nothing - evil. We live evil and or live in evil each and every day and to disturb our nest would be wrong. And this too is sad because there is a better world out there. A world void of violence and strife, sickness and poverty, pain and heartache; stress and sins. The wealth of this world is not like the wealth of this world (earth). Hence this world many cannot comprehend.
Many cannot find.

Many (billions) cannot go due to our constant sins – evils; ills.

Earth – the people of earth has and have become lawless, hence the lawless societies we live in.

**We have no respect for Good God and Allelujah here on earth hence we** *__cannot have respect for him in his abode. Every law he has and have given us to keep we break; hence we side with evil – the devil as you call him against him Good God and Allelujah.__*

__The world of sin suits billions just fine because in this world the god that resides over many of you kill. Hence it is written in your book of sin, lies and deceit. This book you call holy, hence it's your holy bible; holy book of lies. But yet in all that your god command you not to do you do. You are disobedient and disrespectful hence your god tolerate this and is okay with this. And this is sad because at the end of the day, Sodom and Gomorrah is with man and man will be destroyed. Thus saith the Lord thy God meaning it is so.__

I don't know because my dream world is weird. I now have to contend with female evil because male evil was defeated in 2013 hence the games I guess. Female darkness comes.
To me she is the leader of the spiritual church and I truly don't want her in my life because I truly don't want or need anything to do with her church. I shun the whore houses of death; wicked and evil people hence I refuse her. I cannot live my life unclean nor can I live my life like the dead but yet she baffles me. I am confused when it comes to her. I need good and true life. Positive life hence I need to grow, grow up and glow in goodness and in truth. White we say is pure but white is dead; death - pure evil in the spiritual world. Hence I have to live clean. I have to be clean because neither the physical nor the spiritual world is for me because of death, hardships, heartache and pain.

I forsake these worlds in all truth. In all that is good and true, I forsake the physical and spiritual world due to death and sorrow in both worlds. I need a world void of all death and pain – sin. Hence I must rise up in true peace and harmony to the realm of true truth and happiness, true peace and harmony, true hope and true love and that is my realm; the realm Good God and I created for self and our true and good people.

I refuse the realm of evil and I refuse the realm of man. There is no happiness of truth in these worlds; hence I do not choose any of them. I choose and will forever choose Good and Truth over evil; all that is evil. Hence this dream this morning September 22, 2014.

Dreamt I was watching someone I know. She's a singer. I also know this person in reality - the real world. I was seeing her through her window and she was with this younger man - not her husband. She was laughing happily whilst lying on her back. This young man came into her bedroom and he had long eyelashes on. People the eye lashes were tall. They looked like false eyelashes that you put on, but she was happy with him and I wondered where her husband was. If he was dead for her to be with this guy. I don't know what happened next but they hooked me up on a blind date with a Babylonian female. She was Indian Babylonian people. Suffice it to say I did not go on the date with her. I got angry and ended up calling the Babylonian female a dog. And please do not draw the correlation with Jesus calling the Samaritan woman or whatever her lineage is to me calling this woman a dog in my dream. After calling her a dog, I felt bad and wanted to apologize but did not get a chance to because she was hurt by me calling her a dog and she left.

I went to find her (the singer and her mate that set me up on the blind date). I went to her place where she lived. She had lived above a store in the Malton region. When I got to her place her mother was there but she was not home so I left. Leaving I met up on this woman that was angry because it seems this singer and her mate were to meet her for a date and she did not show up. They stood her up. She said she was going to tell her pastor and I told her not to, to let it go and I was on my way again in search of my foes who set me up on a blind date with a female Babylonian.

When we did meet up she knew what had happened as she was dressed in white, a white dress. I was still angry because after a bit of talking I told the Babylonian female who was wearing curly curls now and or curly weave to hide her appearance to make her seem black of mixed lineage faze me. But she did not fool me she was still Babylonian despite her disguise. I told my foe (blind date setter upper) I was tired of these women stealing our men. The conversation continued with me getting upset and saying some choice words. My foe (blind date setter upper) was shocked because she said, "I thought you were clean." People I even said the F word which shocked the Babylonian female because she never knew I swore. At the end, I ended up apologizing to the Babylonian female and she said she had forgotten about it. It was like out of sight and out of mind to her. I wanted to tell her she should not be this way but I didn't get the chance to.

I also had this folded newspaper in my hand and I hit the Babylonian female on the butt with it as if saying another time and I am beginning to like you.

Weird dream hence I am so confused. Like I said my foe (blind date setter upper) was dressed in white and she said I asked for this and or she thought this was what I wanted, what I asked for.

Wow because it matters not my sexual orientation but it matters who I lay with and a Babylonian is not one of my choice of people to lay with or have any form of sexual relations with.

Been there done that in my younger days before my calling. Now that I am called; Babylonians are not on my list of people to date and it matters not if you are Black, White, Indian or Chinese Babylonian. I also do not care if you are a mixture of Black and Indian. You are still a Babylonian and I refuse to date any of you. I don't even want you in my land because your God is not my God, hence we can never be friends. Your God is death hence the cow is worshipped and accepted as being holy by the lots of you.

In my land, the land of truth the cow - rolling cow that comes with fire represents evil in its purest form. In my land when some wicked and evil people die, their spirit turns into a rolling cow that has fire. So the cow to us is not good but evil; of hell and that is why it comes with fire when it wants to kill you. ***True evil must come with fire hence Moses went on the mount and evil gave him his commandments. That fire and or burning bush Moses was talking to is fire and anyone that is of life and the true light of Good God and Allelujah knows this. Know that evil came to Moses in the*** *form of a burning bush. Hence Good God's children can tell you all about evil thus the symbolisms of man - Pagans are wrong.*

Further, please do not have any preconceived notions of me because like I've said and will say again, I am one to pick up Good God and Allelujah and put him to one side and say, hon I've got this and rib you in the onholiest of words. I refuse certain things in my life and if you are not a part of my world and the world of Good God and Allelujah, then truly don't come around me because I truly do not want or need you in my world. LEARN AND KNOW; WHERE NO BONES ARE PROVIDED NO DOGS ARE INVITED. I refuse man's immigration policy when it comes to my kingdom and world of truth. Undesirables stay the bleep out infinitely and indefinitely forever ever without end.

You are not of my God then don't want or need access to the world and or land and lands he has and have given me. The doors are closed to outsiders, so if you are a devil worshipper and you love death, truly stay the hell away from me. My world is not your world, so want and need nothing to do with me just as how I want and need nothing to do with you.

You can keep your lands of death and I will keep my land and lands of truth and true love. I don't want and need your friendship. Hence all I do for the goodness and truth of me and my people including Good God and our people, I do to stay away from you. I do all not to build my home next to you, but build my home infinite and indefinite universes away from you. You cannot reach me in my world because you truly do not know where my world is; hence we will never have beef and or strife. I truly don't want you to find me hence I do all to lose you.

What evil do and does to his people is the concern of evil and not mine. You are not my people so nothing you do to each other concerns me.

You want to die, continue to pay death and go to hell and die. Hell is not my world and kingdom hence I refuse to step foot in hell and save any of you. You are the devil's children and whatever way he decides to punish you is his and hers alone. Your punishment in hell do not concern me and my God hence I will not dirty myself for any of you. You chose death on earth hence locking your soul and or spirit in hell. You made your choice to die on earth so truly live in your hell in hell. Do not expect me to save you because Good God and Allelujah including Death has my word of truth that I will save none of you. This isn't Noah's Ark and time when according to your book of sin Noah told the people to prepare for rain and they laughed at him. I will not come into lands and take Good God's people out. If you refuse to listen and prepare – come out of Babylonian lands the onus is on you. You will be left the hell behind. I refuse to preach to anyone for their own damned good and they don't listen. If you do not want to listen to the truth and adhere to the truth too bleeping bad for you. Go down in flames with the rest of the people (billions) that are hell bound. You did not want better for yourself. However, if you do not have the means to help you and I have the financial means to help you then I must do right by you and help you in this way. But I will only save Good God's people – his true people – the Jews. Not Babylonian Jews but his true people – the true Jews. We've been through hell and back hence I leave death to his and her own.

My boundaries are set, hence I seek ways to flee from man and his wretched world of lies and deceit; condemnation. I am trying to make my life clean hence negative people and energy I do not want nor do I need around me or in my life.

This woman (my foe) told me I am clean. But what she did - setting me up with a Babylonian female was not nice, it was wrong. I am not a Babylonian lover or supporter, so for her to do this was disrespectful and infinitely and indefinitely wrong. For her to set me up with an Indian Babylonian is highly disrespectful because their God is not my God and will infinitely and indefinitely forever ever never ever will be my God.

I do not condone death. I refuse death on every level of life hence death and I could never ever be friends. To this B***h (my foe) you are of hell, an duppy noa who fi frighten and you cannot frighten me. Just as I have to uphold the laws of truth you have to also. I did not ask you to set me up with anyone hence I do hope death deals with you accordingly for disrespecting my life and truths in the physical and spiritual world.

Know this. I know what I want and need out of life and I refuse you and your offer. I refuse you trying to throw me off my path of righteousness and truth. You are not worth it; hence I will not give in to you. Your set up did not work hence I so have to be careful in the waking and or physical world. I have to do me and be me.

I have to wait until the true ordained one comes along, hence I have to cancel my bar date with my niece. I accepted her invitation to a gay bar and I have to cancel after this dream because this is not the avenue he Good God and Allelujah want or need me to travel in. Yes I so wanted to go but I truly cannot because the bar scene is so not for me. I never found them appealing nor do my guides hence this is their warning unto to me to stay out of bars and gay bars. If I go I will lose my cleanliness and I cannot afford this. I am on the road of truth hence I cannot go on the road of lies, whoredom and deceit. *(The pickup people and nothing else so do not get it twisted because I mentioned gay bars. No bar scene is permitted for me or anyone that is walking a clean and true road).*

Yes I would like someone in my life but I have to wait for that person. When he Good God and Allelujah say he's ready, he will send me the right and truthful, positive and clean, honest and good – truly good someone.

Yes it's a waiting game I guess, but I can't wait any longer because I am so not getting any younger. It's not so much intimacy but finding the right and special person; soul mate that you can talk to and relate to. Yes intimacy will play a part but doing things that surrounds nature and water - natural and or things of nature is critical.

Yes I am strange but hey this is me.

Going back to spiritualism, I find every culture is based on the same

nastiness. It's funny because I was looking at Yoruba spiritualism and find it no different from Christianity and the religions of the world. All have the same principle of nastiness (Incest) hence I truly have to ask Africans, where do they truly come from?

How can you as Africans believe in nastiness and say you are true, the center and hub of life when you truly do not know your roots? You truly do not know the center and hub of life – Africa.

Hence Babylon is rooted in Africa and nowhere else.

Many things Africans have adopted and in truth, many cannot trace their lineage further than two to three thousand years ago and this is sad.

All many have is the bible - handed down traditions of lies, sin and evil and this is sad. Hence I cannot comprehend how Africans say they are Africans, but yet have not the truth; the truth of life?

If life started in Africa why aren't Africans living life?

Why are Africans killing self and walking in the way of the dead?

People, I truly don't know, hence I must walk before death like I was told by the one of the two white men in blue long ago.

Death does not concern me because I realize and will forever tell you, we ready accept lies and live by lies hence man - humanity knows not the truth. We would rather kill and die for lies - the devil, rather than live for the truth and live.

We kill for death without knowing death is going to kill us in the end. We do not think of the spiritual realm because we all think life stops when the flesh can no longer breathe and this is sad. We've forgotten about the spirit. Life does not stop at the flesh, it stops at the spirit. Hence there is hell for the wicked and the abode of Good God for the good and pure in heart; the just.

Hell was not created or designed by God or death. Hell was created and designed by man - each and every individual based on the sins you do on a daily basis. Hence good and clean cannot mingle with unclean; the dead.

As humans we are unclean and this is why he Good God cannot mingle with us. His world is not our world because we refuse to change our dirty linen of self. We refuse to wash ourselves clean hence death comes.

We all know **_"the wages of sin is death"_** but we continue to sin anyway. Once the spirit leaves the body then true death comes for some and true live begins for others.

Know this. Good God does not take anyone, death does. It is death we see when the spirit leaves the body not Good God. Come on now.

It matters not if you are good or evil. When the time comes for the spirit to leave its prison (body) death is whom you see and will see. Some people do not see life hence they go down to hell; their downward triangle. And it is beyond me why anyone would want to live in the living for death.

Why would anyone want to go to hell and live in the fires of hell; burn?

But like I said, it's the choice you made. None of us thought of hell and or the time of death. Everyone thinks the mark of the beast is 666 but the mark of the beast is not 666 it is 6666 which totals 24. 24000 years hath the devil to deceive man and the devil has and have won. Shortly (before 2032) man - humans are going to die on a massive scale globally and we cannot blame anyone but self. We accepted the offerings of death hence man live to kill - die.

Humans were not supposed to die. Human flesh and spirit were to return to Good God and Allelujah as one not separate. But because of sin both must be separated.

For some, the spirit is sentenced and judged while for the good; pure in heart, they go up to be cleaned so that they can meet Good God and Allelujah and live forevermore.

Michelle Jean
September 22, 2014 and December 05, 2014

As I come to a close yet again with this book, know that there will be more like this book if time permits.

They will also be in this size and of the same cover.

Listen suffering is for a time and yes it's unfortunate that we have to live this way, but it is our reality because we are governed by a higher power. But with that said, many of us have given up that higher power to live in sin and fancy free.

With death there are no consequences because he did not make the rules. Sin offered and we took.

Sin said this is my game accept or reject it. Many (billions) have accepted it hence billions must be punished. Die.

Yes this is sad because death (sin) did not level the playing field. He did not tell you of his consequences hence look at the world today. But in fact this is a lie because we were specifically told, "the wages (pay) of sin is death."

We are without privacy because technology have and has taken our private life and or privacy away from us. On any given day a hacker can hack into your computer or laptop and watch you do the nasty. They can steal your identity but in truth I refuse to blame all on the hackers. There should be no back doors to your personal information and computer.

There should be no back doors for hackers to get in.

There should be no front or side doors either, but somehow we blame everything on hackers without knowing that some of these major corporations do the hacking. Pay someone to hack you.

Without hackers and viruses these major corporations could not sell you their bogus security features that do not work. So all that is being said and done means naught to me. No company is anyone's friend when it comes to selling their product and services; bogus and false technology that take your right and rights from you.

No one is safe hence the technology of man is bogus and means not a damned thing.

Nothing is safe anymore, hence staying a top the game means nothing to me. You cannot stay atop thieves whose main purpose is to steal all from you. Hence hackers will hack and corporations will make money on their so called internet security.

Yes this is a shame but this is how society is run. It is being run by thieves that cannot see the bigger picture. All are looking for profitability, the bottom line. All are looking to the future for hope and salvation and truly do not know that there is no future for them. It's going to be a survival game real soon, hence billions will not see beyond 2032 and it's a crying shame.

In all we did, we say we want and need a future and or a better life but have done nothing to preserve our future to have a better life; tomorrow.

Like I've said, we say we are civilized but we are not. We live to kill hence we do kill and disobey the commandments of God - Good God and Allelujah. We broke his commandments not Moses. Hence your book of sin lied to you when it said Moses broke them; the commandments of God.

We are the ones that cannot live clean hence we disobey and commit adultery.

We kill each other. War

We covet our neighbours home, wife, husband; all.

We steal (have no privacy).

We lack morals hence we glorify sin; violent movies and video games; immorality all around. Yes the whores of Hollywood that undresses for the public and world to see. They teach and preach immorality and the world gobble this up in praise and admiration without thinking that they too have to pay for their wrongs; evils. What the people of the world and these celebrities have forgotten is that children are seeing their immoral behaviours and emulating them. These whores and slores of Hollywood have children and none consider the reputation of these children; their children. Nor do they consider the future of their children. Hence Sodom and Gomorrah is in full swing in the United States of America. We were told in the last days people will be lovers of themselves; they would worship vanity and so said, so done. This is the last of days hence the extinction of humanity globally before 2032. As human beings we do not think, but now we have to think because death comes to collect his pay on a massive scale shortly. Many who are doing this are not thinking of the consequences. Many say they are not hurting anyone but you are hurting someone. You are hurting yourself, children globally as well as your family. Look at the image you are painting for yourself and the world to see. More importantly, look at the image you are showing Good God and Death of yourself. ALL THOSE PHOTOS AND MOVIES DEATH HAS IN YOUR RECORD BOOK OF SIN. YOU CANNOT GET AWAY FROM THIS JUDGMENT BECAUSE DEATH HAS YOU TAGGED IN THE NUDE, YOUR NUDE SELFIES YOU SELL ON THE INTERNET AND IN MAGAZINES. You cannot get away from this because you gave death ammunition against you each and every day, hence your lack of morals and self respect for self and others. You sell yourself as well as your children and family for profit; the dollar bill and Satan himself. Therefore the lack of morals and values in this society of whoredom and prostitution – Hollywood. The goodness of life is not valued, hence Good God cannot be found in the places of evil. He cannot be found in bars, churches of whoredom and immorality, immoral lands, the hospitals of death nor can he be found in the homes of these actors and actresses because none know him, they sell evil, live and dine in evil; do all that is wicked and evil.

We do all that we are not to do. So how come we blame Moses for breaking Good God's commandments when Moses did nothing wrong? Know this, if Moses broke the commandments of God – Good God we would not have them today. Humanity would not be around today. All would have been lost – destroyed long ago and we would cease to exist. Like I said, we are the ones to break every commandment of God – Good God and we are the ones that are going to become extinct before 2032.

Now I ask you this. Are we not the devil's own because none of God's – Good God's commandments we can obey?

We listen to people say kill and everything will be okay because someone is going to redeem your life and or soul for you and this is not true. No one can redeem your soul for you if you are the one to do wrong. You must redeem your own soul by coming clean and this is what we fail to realize as humans.

No one can die to save you from your sins. Nor can anyone die to pay for your sins. Your sins are your sins because you commit them not the next man or person commit them for you. Good God and Allelujah is life and he would never ever beyond a shadow of a doubt let his children die for wicked and evil people. He's given us laws and we are the ones to break them without thinking of the consequences. When we do this, we are basically telling him Good God bleep him when we disobey. So why would he save you and or any of us if we constantly disobey him and have no respect for the law and laws he has and have given us.

Each and every day we break his commandments then have the nerve to say someone is going to die to save you; us. Please there are no scapegoats in God's kingdom hence you are all scapegoats for death. Death is going to kill you. This is your reality and no one can get away from this. Hence death is in the physical and spiritual. Come on now.

Like I've said, Good God and Allelujah infinitely do not deal in unclean. So why do we think he would save us when we do not listen to him? We break his every law and or all his laws - commandments he's given us so why should he save us?

We know better but yet refuse to do better.

In all we do, we want someone to die for us. Be our sacrificial lamb and that is not right. Do for you and live because the life you save will be your own.

And I will repeat so that Death, Good God and Allelujah and all of humanity know. If I am the saving grace for the people of this earth, I refuse to save anyone that is wicked and evil. I will indefinitely and forever ever never ever save any because wicked and evil people know that what they were doing is wrong. Hence the spiritual world does not like me and I truly don't give a damn. You cannot constantly hurt people and expect to get away with it. Come on now. We gave Satan the victory over us because we listened to the lies of the church – clergies of the world. And now that time is winding down we are looking for a shield and a scapegoat to save us.

We gave Satan the victory over us because we listened to the lies of others; his people.

Not because we are not punished right away does not mean that we are not going to be punished. We are going to be punished hence 666 is time, the time to die. Eve didn't die right away in physical and we all know this and it's the same for us. She had no saving grace because she disobeyed hence billions of you today have no saving grace just like Eve (Evening). You went against the laws of life and death. You did not heed the consequences of your sinful actions and now it's time to divvy up globally.

I refuse to save anyone that is wicked and evil in the spiritual world either. The devil's children are not my keep and will never be. Hence the devil's children I have to do all to stay away from.

What belongs to death belongs to him and I refuse to interfere with him and his people anymore. Like I said, they are not my concern and never will be. Good God's good, true, clean, positive and just children are my concern and forever will be.

I have to live my life no matter how hard it is and or gets and they have to live theirs. Evil people are the ones to choose evil over good and you cannot choose evil over good. You must choose good over evil because there is no life at the end of evils time just death.

Hence my world and kingdom must be built infinitely and indefinitely away from them; all who are wicked and evil. Nor can they (wicked and evil spirits and people) find my place. Just like how they cannot find Good God.

Michelle Jean
September 22, 2014

It's September 27, 2014 Good God and my thoughts are neither here nor there. It's on a different level because of what I read on the internet September 26. Hence I voiced my concerns to you. I so want to walk away from you because I cannot see you in all of this. *I cannot deal with so much hate and I should not have to.*

All I see and read is hate. I know some of my writings can be racist but I tell you and my readers when they are; I'm being racist. I make no apologies for my words in these books hence I stand by them as well as stand by you; but there comes a time when you truly have to let go.

The hate has to stop Good God, it has to because the pain is real and I truly cannot take the pain and hate anymore. Like I said, I tell you and my readers when I am being racist but to have someone call another race – the black race shit then I draw the line. Shit is something that we pass and for someone to say another race is this – shit, I have to draw the line with you.

I know I've called other god's shit and say we've (the black race) have become the dung of the earth – society but I know what I am talking about. We the black race are fed garbage and thought of as garbage; nothing by all the races of earth including our own.

I know the smell of death, the death of wicked and evil people. When they are going to die they, not all emit the smell of feces literally. The smell of poop surrounds them and no matter how the person takes a shower they cannot get rid of that foul smell – odor. So I know but to actually call another race shit – the black race shit I draw the line.

Yes I know slavery is and was a part of our nasty history because we gave up our rich heritage and rights to life and become a part of the devil's own. Because of our actions it cost us our place with you and this is truly sad.

It cost us our lives.

It cost us our future and prosperity so yes I know. We were the ones to choose death. (Adam and Eve)

We disobeyed and got cast out.

We still refuse to listen. Hence we are like our ancestors of old that listened to evil (the Babylonians) Northern Tribes People. Many lost their lives because they died spiritually and physically. Now man is slated to die physically and spiritually again. Yes we caused our own destruction because we would not listen and we are still doing the same thing today – not listening.

Different races – societies have and has colonized us, hence we are misguided, confused; broken. And in truth Good God, I cannot take this broken life anymore. We need to repair self as well as repair the damage done in earth; to earth and in our lives infinitely and indefinitely forever ever without end in a good, true, clean, honest and positive way. We have

to be just with self and others; but we cannot do this in an unjust and lawless society. Hence I cannot take the hatred based on hue; human – the hue of man (skin colour) anymore.
I cannot take the hatred based on religious affiliations – greed anymore.

I cannot take the hatred based on religious lies anymore.

I cannot take the hatred based on sexual preference and lies (transgenderism) anymore.

I cannot take the hatred based on eye colour and hair type anymore.

I cannot take the hatred based on size. What you tell me the normal body size is anymore.

I cannot take the lies nor can I take the environmental killings and hatred anymore.

No form of hatred can I take anymore. In all that we do, we kill life and I truly cannot take it anymore. Everywhere is death, death, death and I cannot take it. Let death be done already. Death has and have prepared a place for his and her people, let them truly take their own and leave forever ever never to come back to earth ever again. The death nonsense must stop because true life needs to begin. Positive and good life must reign forever more without end more than indefinitely.

I cannot take the loving so anymore no matter how great loving us so is. I need true love hence you are truly not the God for me when it comes to loving us so. You cannot give true, you can only give so. Hence I've been fooling and killing myself all along. True love does not cause pain, hence I have to go back to Bob Marley when he said, "how good and or great it would be to see the unification of all Africans – Rasta man?" I realize I do need this – the unification of my people in a good and true way. We need this true unification so that we can live in true peace without the lies of our enemies. ***Good God all was taken from us including you and all you've done to save us we've failed you and you have and has failed us. You failed to communicate properly with us hence we continue to fail you in all that we do. We accepted other gods and the devil did bruise us even killed us. Hence he tied our feet whilst ensuring we go to hell and die.*** You knew this would happen but yet let it happen anyway. You have not put forth your full effort in helping man and this is sad. ***Yes I know the reasoning behind your nature. We fail to listen to the truth. Instead of accepting the truth we accept lies and say they (these lies) are the truth.*** This is sad yes but you could have tried harder. You allowed the devil to infiltrate our lands hence killing hundreds of millions globally. Now billions are going to die. And to be honest with you, in all I do to convince you; I truly cannot put the blame on you because as humans we knew the deceit and lies of Sin – Satan. ***Despite their book being the book of sin, lies and deceit; this book did show all of humanity how Satan deceived Eve and lied to her.*** Sin was held at bay – could not get to your people but one allowed evil in and it is still costing us until this day. This is why I tell you Good God and Allelujah that once death takes his people to never ever let any form of evil come back into our new kingdom and world; earth. Under no circumstances must evil be let in ever again. I don't care how good they seem in the end, we cannot lay ourselves careless to let them in again. Hence I tell you now, if you know one good person in our lot that is going to have compassion for anyone one of them – Satan's children; to not let that person in infinitely and indefinitely without end. I refuse to live in the heartache and pain; sorrow of sin again. Too many lives have and has been lost. Nor is it fair to earth; the waterways of earth, the animals, air and trees of earth to put up with the evils of man and spirit again. Good God look how many trees we've cut down and have not replaced.

Look how many animals that have become extinct because of the evils of man and their evil society. In all that man – humanity has and have done, they never thought of their true self, the spirit and the other lives of earth including earth.

Wow. We think the living on earth is hell, trust me you haven't faced hell yet.

Allelujah, dear God they truly don't know what they are going to face in hell because of their sins. Hence it's panic time because the end is truly near for billions globally real soon. So in all your doing Good God, truly hide your people from sin once this is done and even before death takes his people. Good God, remember it was Adam and Eve that was kicked out of the Garden of Eden not the rest of your people. You made sure you sealed the passage way of life and truth from Adam and Eve. Hence I tell you to save your people; those that are true and good to you; clean. Save them from what is to come and put another seal that man cannot find infinitely and indefinitely around them so that no one can find us just like you did when you locked Adam and Eve out. Good God, we truly do not need to see death nor do we need to be amongst death's people and children. So if it be thy will, please let my asking of you be good and true to you in all that I do and ask of thee.

Onwards I go because I know Good God, I know, I know, I know. Dear God I know hence woe be unto man – his and her spirit when death is done literally.

Yes it would be great for blacks to be unified but in all I need, hope and dream, I realize that you Good God is not unified with me or in me the way I need you to be.

Am I hurt?

Yes I am. When I read the comments on the internet of this person saying our race is shit I thought of you. He said we are shit hence that makes you Good God and Allelujah shit too. Hence I cannot walk with you on this hate train and hate road anymore. _**Good God for a**_ *product (internet) that was mean to bring societies of different cultures together this product (internet) has only helped in spreading hate. The greatest platform for any form of hate is the internet.* Hence the internet is like the churches of the globe – evil. Yes this is unfortunate for me to say this but where is the better good in this product when I read more hate and see people disgracing self. Hence I would like to have my own platform (television station and or video blog) whichever you permit me to do because I have an idea of what I would truly love to do and this platform. Trust me this platform will be true to you and me.

Onwards I go again.

As a black woman and human being, I have to have ambition and pride for myself and for my own. I have to respect myself and my own and you have to do the same. Yes I cuss out some but that's me when anger sets in.

In all I've done, I've tried to justify self – this comment and compare it to what I've written (racist comments) but I truly cannot. Nothing can justify another human being calling another race – the race of blacks shit. They are classing you Good God as shit hence they've classed your people as shit. Yes the dream above of me calling a Babylonian a dog. I will not justify my actions because I too have done wrong. Hence I truly have to walk away from you and let you open the door for someone else (her) to save humanity. I cannot save humanity in good and true faith; hope due to true hurt and pain; the classing of you and your people as shit. The hatred of man is too much for me to bare hence I draw the line and walk away from you and it all. This hate touched home and that home is you and me. Hence I keep telling you to have ambition of self. People do not choose you so leave them the hell alone. If I am telling you get lost then truly get lost and do not return. Save your true people from the flood – harvest that's to come globally. Prepare a true and good place for them where they are save from this deadly storm. The storm is here hence let your people escape without the devil knowing. Let them flee to you in truth. You have to do this for them so truly hear me when I talk to you and move on. We are the ones to divorce you and accept death – the devil, so truly leave us to burn because we chose hell's fire and not you.

I draw the line with all this Good God because if I had my way, I would save no one in humanity given what I read and see on the internet and in reality; the real world. We humans are the unjust and vile ones because we cannot live good with anyone or anything. Hence I truly step aside from you and death and let you both handle your business; affairs when it comes to life and death – humans.

Both sides are wrong hence I leave both sides to your own demise. I truly cannot fight for a God that has no life and ambition for self and others; his and her people.

I cannot fight for a God that has no true love for himself.

I cannot fight for a God that has no true love for the environment, animals, waterways, air and trees of the land; Mother Earth.

I truly love nature because I see the beauty of life in the trees, but you cannot see this Good God. You allow people to kill this beauty (the beauty of the trees). Hence I have to be true to me and the environment; Earth and all the goodness of earth. The hatred of man is not called for, hence all you did, you did not do out of truth. You did all for man to destroy hence she told me God kills. And given the nature of humans (humanity) globally; she is not wrong (false) in her saying. She is correct in telling me this. You permit evil to destroy truth; all that is good and true and you are wrong in doing so because life – good life is worth it. But if you have no life morals – goodness in you, how can man and or humanity have goodness and truth; morals in them?

I truly love you yes, but I cannot knowingly stay with someone that cannot truly love me and his people; the earth on a whole and the true and good universe. Good God, we need you but you've proven to me that you do not need us and this is sad. We are looking to you for truth in all that we do, so truly stand by your own. Stand up for us and hold on to us. We need this, I surely and truly do.

You cannot sit on the sidelines and watch us die. Maybe I live in a fantasy world when it comes to you. Maybe I am too clingy to you. Maybe what I am expecting of you, you cannot truly give to me and this is sad. But in all that I do, it's not about me and me alone, it's about us and the people – family that I hold dear to me and you; your people who are my people, this earth and universe.

Maybe I trust you and truly love you too much but I cannot help this. This is me. I cannot hold back when it comes to you. I refuse to and maybe this is my downfall when it comes to you but in all truth, I truly do not want or need to see you hurt despite it all.

In all that I do, I truly cannot stay with you any longer because you see the hatred of your people and instead of lifting them up to meet you, you leave them in sorrow; pain. You allowed evil to take all from us including our dignity. We lost you and I am not okay with this because you've always been our right and you let evil take our right – you from us.

You allow the devil's own to class us as shit hence classing you as shit. Tell me how am I to take this? How am I to feel?

How am I to live with this? You are the creator of all but yet humanity respects you not. Hence I cannot stay with a God that lacks ambition for self, the universe, earth and his true people. So because of what I read on September 26, 2014, I truly cannot go into lands that truly hate my people. I also have to walk away from you because you lack truth and ambition for self – you. I have to have ambition for me and my people, hence I truly have to let Russia, Iceland, Greenland, Spain, France and Scotland go. Yes it's painful but I have to deal with my hurt my way. As humans we do not like to be hurt but when it comes to others we truly do not care.

Yes this may seem two sided because of what I said about wicked and evil people, but it truly is not. I am letting wicked and evil people go. I will not save them because of the hurt and pain they've knowingly and willingly cause others. Many build weapons to kill other people and I cannot accept this nor can Good God because that person is willingly and knowingly taking away from life.

Many design and create diseases in laboratories to kill other human beings on a massive scale all because of profit – greed; financial gain and stability and I cannot accept this nor can Good God.

Many kill for sport; all because they are a part of a gang and I cannot accept this nor can Good God and Allelujah. The hurt and pain that is associated with gang violence is great; that painful. These people kill for a place in hell because gangs are of the devil. Satan owns these people literally hence the demonic acts some commit and tattoos that they spread across their bodies and desecrate the flesh.

Yes there is a lot more. So because of this and more, I care not about wicked and evil people – the devil's own. I cannot Good God because they are not your children and people nor are they mine. I will not hate you because of what you do or the lifestyle you choose. I will get angry but in all of my anger, I leave the enemies of God – Good God and Allelujah and his true people including me to time because time is what we have. We are guaranteed the death of all evil and wicked people including spirits in time. No one that is evil can get away with evil because if you don't face hell on earth, hell will not pass you in the grave. So I worry not about my enemies because I truly know hell and the fires of hell that will consume their spirit for their allotted time before their final extinction – death. Let me tell you this. Physical death is not death compared to spiritual torture and death.

The pain we feel here on earth is nothing compared to the pain you will feel in hell. Like I've said in another book, the demons of hell live to inflict pain. And the more you sin is the longer they inflict pain on you in the grave; hell, your new home and resting place. See many don't know that the spirit is your true life that is why no one can kill the spirit in the physical realm. See every human being had a chance to get back in the realm of Good God and Allelujah but refuse to.

Don't go there with the church bullshit and nonsense because if the clergies of the globe knew God – Good God and Allelujah and if they were in fact ordained by God – Good God and Allelujah they would know this and know the truth. Like I said, every human being had a chance, was given a chance to get back in the realm of God – Good God and Allelujah but instead of accepting the truth and live clean, we choose unclean instead. We choose death and sin over goodness and truth; cleanliness. So because we choose death all the time over goodness and truth; cleanliness, we cannot find Good God nor can we reside with him because we are not <u>**CLEAN.**</u> <u>**Also, because of your unclean state you cannot save your loved ones in the grave and this is truly sad for many of you.**</u>

Life is not death and no one can die to see God – Good God and Allelujah and I've told you this over and over again. Like I said, if you can stomach it, look at a dead body. That body hath not life, so if you do not have life how can you live? You are dead just like that dead body. You are void of all life hence revelations said, you were the first begotten of the dead because you believe in a dead God; Jesus. So because you believe in a dead god and worship a dead god you became dead like him. Come on now.

Hate, I loathe and despise and from you despise me – the race of shit as we are called by one on the internet, I truly cannot in good faith and truth save any of you. Yes this pains me but the one did affect hundreds of millions and it's a true shame. I truly love your lands but I cannot go amongst people that truly loathe me and my people including my God, the God – True God of Life – Truth. Hence whatever God – Good God and Allelujah including Death wants to do with you is no longer my concern. I have to truly walk away; step aside in goodness and in truth. No one was put on this earth to hate or be hated but yet we hate anyway.

No one was put on this earth to die but yet we live to die – kill anyway.

No one was put on this earth to be controlled and dominated by anyone but yet we see it befitting to control and dominate anyway. We do not think of the pain we've caused but I am. And no, I will not make any apologies for any of the words in these books like I've said.

Every nation has and have stolen from the black man's history and culture and made it theirs. So if we are shit, why steal from us?

Why vacation in the lands of shit?

Why marry our women because we are shit?

Why talk to us because we are shit?

Leave our bleeping black men and women alone because we are shit. You should have nothing to do with the race of shit. And don't bleeping want our men's sperm either. And no, you can't have our eggs because our eggs and sperm including blood is shit; so you shouldn't want or need it.

Don't want our diamonds and oil because these precious commodities are shit because they come from the land and lands of shit – the shit people.

Don't listen to our music and wear our clothes because they are shit too. It's the race of shit that wears them and makes them as well as makes the music you listen to. So you should not want and need what we have because they are shit.

Don't bleeping come in contact with us because we are shit – the race of shit as classed by one of you on the internet.

Don't ask us to buy your money or invest in your companies because we are shit, so our money is shit too.

So to you, because you classed the race of blacks as shit, then stay the bleep out of Africa and don't invest your money in our land and lands because our land and lands are shit.

Don't sell us your products and services either because we are shit.

Don't sell us your commodities because we are shit.

Do not dance like us and try to be like us because we are shit hence our dance is shit too.

Don't swag like us because our swag is shit.

Don't cane row your hair like us because cane row comes from the people of shit hence you should not wear cane row; rock it on your heads.

Don't tan your skin to look like us because we are the race of shit as classed by one of you, so tanning your skin to look like the race of shit is infinitely and indefinitely not permitted forever ever without end indefinitely.

Don't use any of our inventions either because it was the race of shit that invented:
The Carbon Filament Light Bulb - Lewis Latimer
The Cataract Laserphaco Probe – Patricia Bath
The Artificial Heart Pacemaker Control Unit – Otis Boykin
The Mutiplex Telegraph – Granville T. Woods
The Modern Home – Video Gaming Control – Gerald A. Lawson
3D Graphics Technology Used in Films – Marc Hannah
Traffic Lights
The trees and waterways of earth
The universe

Life itself is black owned and created. So because we the race of shit as classed by you and we invented it all, get yourself and your race the bleep off earth because we designed and created it all. Find your own damned dead planet Mars or whatever planet you come from and truly get the bleep lost.

We are the true creators so create your own and truly leave us the hell alone asshole.

Do not bleeping adopt our children either because these children come from shit so they are shit too.

Don't worship and praise our God either because he is

shit. Hence he created people that are shit hence the universe is shit and his planet that he designed and create that you free load off is shit too. So truly get the bleep off earth and find your own damned planet. Oops you can't find one because your God did not create any hence he too is free loading off my God, the one that you classed as shit.

Don't celebrate our holidays either because these holidays are shit too.

Don't celebrate our customs either because these customs are shit.

You want nothing to do with us the shit race then bleeping leave us the bleep alone. I certainly don't want or need you in Good God's new kingdom. Hence in the name of God, Good God and Allelujah, I lock you and all the people of your country eternally out of Good God's Kingdom and abode infinitely and indefinitely forever ever without end because I'm shit, he Good God and Allelujah is shit and his people is shit too. So truly don't want to come into our world and worlds that we are building. We are shit hence his shit people will stand with him, praise him and continue to truly love him unconditionally in spirit and in truth; the physical and spiritual forever ever without end infinitely and indefinitely. Whatever goodness he Good God and Allelujah bless us with from now on, truly want none for you and your people because you will get none. And I am truly hoping that Good God will approve my request in all goodness and truth not just for me and his people but for him also. Damn rude an wrenk. Buoy if mi cuss yu hell tun up and fiya blaze hatta. Truly go and find yourself before mi cuss yu like there is no tomorrow. Truly look at the black race because we are perfection not bleeping death like you to be racist. We are well defined and well cooked so clear off and find your god Satan and let him show you what shit is because I am sure he will show you shit and that is bleeping you.

Let me tell you this, the black race needs none of you. We need no other race; you all bleeping need us. Know this, the day we all die is the day you and earth dies. We the black race keeps the earth revolving. We the black race is the ones to keep every race on the face of this planet alive until this day. It was out of our blackness that Black God created it all from because there are not bleeping WHITE GODS ONLY WHITE DEATH.

Black people have some bleeping ambition for yourself and people and stop letting others degrade you and ride off your coat tail. I'm fed up of the disrespect by bleeping people that have no bleeping history. Come on now. They can't even find their own bleeping God because they've got none. So respect your damned selves and skin; own. Yes I am being racist because like I've said, some whites are black and some blacks are white. But for the white blacks they will comprehend, understand and over stand because they fall under the banner of black and I truly do not see them as white but black. Yes this is hard to explain if you are not of the spiritual realm; meaning if you know not the spiritual realm. This is why I refuse to hate hence I cuss your ass out rude and proper and put you in your damned place. And I don't give a damn who you are or who likes it; the way I cuss out people.

Every nation has and have colonized us (the black race) and given us their languages, religions of death including their man made diseases and I am tired, truly tired of it all.

I am tired of everything including the god syndrome of death.

A God that truly loves, do all in his or her power to save his and her own. Hence as a child of truth, I have to do all that is good and true, positive and clean to save my Black Own. Yes my African Home and Own. I cannot be like the rest of the black population in the west that have and has made it financially and have done absolutely nothing in truth for their AFRICAN OWN – BLACK OWN. And don't you dare bring up Oprah because if she truly cared she would have a studio in Africa helping her African own.

And don't go there because I know some are saying they don't want to be labeled as African American. This is great because I do hope Good God and Allelujah is taking note of them disassociating themselves from Africa. Hence when Africa returns to its pristine beauty and wealth, I truly hope none will want and need a place in Africa because they are not African Americans. And for those that are saying the black hair is nasty and they hate it, I truly hope when the blessings of God – Good God comes down from the heavens and you get none you will remember you disassociating yourselves from Good God and all that is Black and True; your nappy as pappy hair. For you that do not know. Take a look at the map of the globe. See how America is attached to South America. Now attach South America to Africa. Hence when you are called African American; be honoured and privileged. You heard about the Ameers. Many say they were Arab but they were black – YOU. No one can take your truth from you but you yourself. America is well was a part of Africa before the great separation hence America was black land. Forget slavery because Good God did not make slaves man did. We were told we were taken from Africa, we were not all taken from Africa because BLACK PEOPLE RESIDED IN EVERY CORNER OF THE GLOBE. Know your true history and know the truth. Earth belongs to us and no other. Earth is our right because we are descendents of God – Good God and Allelujah. And yes not all blacks are descendants of God – Good God; some are descendants of Satan, the devil and or death.

Bob Marley told you not to let them school you and fool you but as blacks we fight to be a part of societies that hate and loathe us instead fighting for our own and building our own. They want America, bleeping give America to them because soon America is going to fall and where will many of you blacks be? Many of you that are getting food stamps and medi

– care will not get it because the country will not be able to feed millions of you. Get a clue and leave. Find a way out and find a home in Africa and live come on now. Truly love you. Look at it this way, all your billionaires are going to lose it all because the American Dollar must collapse. This collapse will take the global market with it so China you had better get your books in order and quick as well as have an alternative markets to sell in. Despite the reservations of all, Africa and Russia is there so make good and true choices when it comes to saving your people and having an alternative market. Russia and Africa have things that you need so truly buy from them and look at Canada too. Yes the fall of America is going to affect them but I cannot leave them out despite the way I feel about them. They have softwood lumber, buy from them. Hey Canada has great steel use them as a source if you need steel. Like I said, despite my reservations of them make them a good trading partner as well. Listen I can't let Canada fall with the United States, I have to do to save them.

So for all of you the White Race that are telling black people to go back to Africa know that we are in Africa and America is our home. You just came in and ruined it, stole our birthright just like Jacob did to Esau. We belong more than you. Well not me but black Americans. Not one of you can name a land that truly belongs to you. Don't even go there about European lands because Blacks were in Europe long before you.

India forget it, there are Black Nodites and if you read Genesis you would know that.

China, look at Buddha's head, black man's hair on Chinese skin. And forget it; the Chinese are a part of the Black Race anyway. Though they will dispute this but Good God and Allelujah does not lie dem be black honey. Hence they can be found at the base of Good God's mountain with the black race.

Strayed again but onwards I go.

Some of you players – basketball and baseball players, if you truly loved your African own, you would truly help Africa and Africans in a good and positive way. Slums you would invest money in to clean it up so that your own can look up in pride and say thank you and thank you Good God for helping us; hearing our cries and pleas and seeing our pain. Thank you for remembering us and helping us. Thank you for truly saving us.

Remember many of our ancestors were taken from Africa and made into slaves. So as children of Africans not slaves, why can't we be proud of our own; African own and build our African own positively?

They don't want us in their lands; the land they stole from us as well as the land Good God separated America from, Africa, so why can't we have some ambition and take our money out of their lands and go home to Africa where we belong? Why can't we separate ourselves from them like Psalms One say and go home?

Yes the desert is there but can't we plant corn or cactus trees so that when drought comes we have corn to eat and the water of cactus trees to drink.

Africa has many deserts so why can't we utilize these desert spaces?

The desert is hot. Can we not utilize this heat of the desert in the form of Geo Thermal Energy without the use of geysers and or hot springs?

If we cannot live in the desert why can't we use the desert to our benefit?

The desert doesn't have to be sand. Why can't it be our oasis for good food and trees? Mangoes, Jackfruit, Yams, Cassava, Sugarcane, Turnip; a harvest of a different and positive kind.

What about cotton? Can cotton grow in the desert?

Yes the black race is hated globally and despite me saying I wish I was never black in my anger, I am honoured and proud to be black because I am from the race of God – Good God and Allelujah. I know the devil has his time and I have to leave them (the devil and his people) to time. There is a hell to pay and every wicked and evil comment that is made against the black race and any race for that matter that individual must pay in hell this is guaranteed.

Yes I am his child because his life flows through me in the physical and spiritual realm and I am his choice; the one he chose to write his books. And despite my loneliness and anger at times I know he's there protecting me.

I know hatred is not of Good God hence the downfall of man – humanity real soon. I know I cannot change the hearts and minds of man – humanity and I refuse to. As humans we know better but refuse to do better. We refuse to know that the more we hate it's the further we get from God – Good God and Allelujah and the longer our spirit burns in hell.

We all think life stops at the flesh but life does not stop at the flesh, it stops at the spirit. Hence we were told to live in spirit and in truth.

We are governed by the spirit hence I truly walk away from it all and let life and death take its course – take their own; all. Yes I am stepping aside as of 2015, January 1 and I am so looking forward to this, the new and improved me.

Humanity have and has been found guilty hence the full charcoal black moon I saw. This is our destruction and if I could I would not override this destruction for anyone. Yes I know not all will die, but if you are not a part of the 144 million not 144 thousand, then truly good luck to man – humanity globally real soon. Like I said, if I am the saving grace for humanity, I will not change the course of life and death nor will I save wicked and evil people because evil cannot change. Evil can only die hence man – wicked and evil men and women including spirits is going to die; do die. Also if you do to get, for example, adopt a black child just to be saved, I will infinitely and indefinitely never ever without a shadow of a doubt save you and that child. Nor will Good God and Allelujah save you and that child because you did to get; you weren't true.

I will never ever save you if you marry a black woman or man to have bi-racial children to get into Good God and Allelujah's kingdom. Nor will he Good God and Allelujah save you because you did to get; you weren't true.

So for all of you that are banking on that adoptive black child and or bi-racial relationship and child to get you into Good God's kingdom in the end; truly good luck because you do to get and this is infinitely and indefinitely forbidden; not allowed. Hence truly good luck to billions of you that were banking on this because all the devil told you wasn't true; he or she lied to you.

<u>Death had his time to deceive and death did deceive. Humanity knew the lies and deceit of Sin – Satan. But instead of changing this and living for the truth we continue to sin vile as well as live in sin. Hence your mark of the beast 666 is the time for humans to die. That time has come hence the alarm has sounded and truly woe be unto man globally real soon. Oh add another 6 to the 666 and you will get the true time of death. His one day to deceive and lie to all of you.</u>

<u>Your woes have just begun because the alarm and trumpet has been sounded by me. You were told many will run to the rock (mountain) but the rock will refuse them. Hence many billions will run to God – Good God and will be told too late. I know you not and I refuse you. There is no last minute train or bus so truly good luck in your coming end; end of physical and spiritual life.</u>

Good God is not a God of hate. He's the God of truth and cleanliness. He is just and if your name is not written in his holy book; little book, red book; no not red but burgundy red if that's a colour, then truly good luck because you will not be saved.

A government and nation cannot hate and expect to see and or reside with Good God and Allelujah.

A government and nation cannot cut down the trees of life and expect Good God to find favour in your land. This will never happen because you are destroying life, the trees of life. If you cut one tree down you are to plant two (2) or three (3) to replace that one life (tree) you have taken.

Natural life is valued above all including valued above man because Nature; trees do not kill, man – human does, humans kill trees; all. Hence nature will always have more value than humans because of this. In all we as humans have and has done, we pollute everything then have the gaul to say disease is a part of our DNA – heredity.

Good God made no diseases and no one can say they have seen or can find God – Good God and Allelujah in the laboratories of man and or humanity designing and creating drugs and weapons of mass destruction to kill man; all.

Good God made man disease free. Man is the one to create diseases not God – Good God and Allelujah.

None can say Good God gave them the chemical compounds to destroy and kill another; anyone.

None of this Good God and Allelujah did, but yet we say we are humans – civilized living in civilized societies and are of God – Good God. Life cannot kill, but yet I comprehend her because of what man has done unto man. We design nuclear weapons and germicides; diseases to kill each other. Then wonder why Satan is still alive and living amongst men. Yes some wonder why Satan still roams the earth. Well take a look at the sins of man globally and answer your own question.

We sin. Therefore, because of our sins Satan cannot die. He must walk with his people and tell them what to do. He must let them continue to sin by giving you all you want whilst plunging you further into hell. Once you are in hell truly good luck in getting out because Satan will not let you go. Some of you signed death's contract hence you have to make sacrifices yearly to keep ahead of his game. Hence many of you care not who you kill – sacrifice. When this woman told me God kills I know her God is death because death is a God. Hence death can kill and do kill. Life cannot stand in the way of death. Hence life and death is separate; not the same – different all around. One is negative energy and the other positive energy; life.

Life goes up whilst death go down to death; hell to burn.

Yes billions have and has given their lives over to death foolishly, hence hell's fire; the cow of death; fire that billions worship until this day. Many worship death – the cow – fire hence evil – pure evil will always return fire to his and her own. Hence the golden calf and rolling cow until this day.

We know death and can see death but yet we fail to take heed. We continue to believe in the lies of death and cannot take heed and step aside and let death and evil go.

I have taken heed hence I've stepped aside to let life and death handle his and her own; their own. A civilized society looks at the best interest and the greater good of all not just humanity – humans. All is a part of our eco system. And that all includes the animals of earth, the waterways of earth, the air and trees of earth. But as humans we could not take care of all. We could not cherish and take care of all in a good and true way. We killed all in the name of greed – death, so because of this; we too must be killed; die.

In all that we did to earth, she too (Earth) must be vindicated for the wrongs we as humans have and has done to her. So to all the owners of companies globally that destroys and pollutes the earth, all your sins done to earth is added to your record; sin record. No, I cannot tell you what the value of your sin is but trust me its grave and you will pay in hell for your sins. Trust me as I am writing this, death is adding another page to your book; sin record. You politicians too that have commission bombs to be detonated in her, death is adding another page to your book; sin record.

Everyone that has caused earth to grieve including shed the blood of humans in her knowingly and willingly, death is adding another page to your book; sin record. I cannot help you because you did her (Earth) wrong. Yes there is more but I will leave things at this because you now get the drift. Earth is a part of life; hence Death must include her and her children – trees, waterways, grass, food and animals that we destroy and kill into the grand scheme of things. He Good God must also take Earth into account; consideration hence truly good luck to some of you. Yes I know some of us consume meat. This is fine, but to hunt animals to extinction is not fine. To use them as game in our sick and twisted games is not right. Yes all have life hence we are to respect all life.

As for me, I have to think of all and what is just and fair, true and clean for both worlds; life and death. Hence what belongs to death, death must keep and must take with him and her and go. Go back to his and her world and or worlds; hell and the fires of hell. I cannot stand in death's way nor can I stand in the way of his people. Death has a claim to you and he and she must take his and her own and he Good God and Allelujah cannot stop Death from doing so. You are his right; the right of death if you truly belong to him or her. Death cannot take you if you do not belong to death. Come on now.

And for the many that is saying Massa Gad a Gad and he will save us despite our faults; sins. I will duly remind you yet again, ***"THE WAGES OF SIN IS DEATH."***

You went against the values and morals of God – Good God and Allelujah so you cannot say Massa Gad a Gad and he will save us because he won't.

Good God is strict people and from you side with death you are against him Good God and Allelujah. He leaves you to your own demise and this is what's happening right now. You cannot say you love him and do all to hurt and deceive him.

You cannot say you love him and sing songs to another God.

You cannot say you love him and turn around and praise and worship death.

You have to be true to him and him alone because he is the one sustaining and maintaining you not death.

You cannot say you love him and make sacrifices unto death come on now.

Living in lies is not living in truth.

Worshipping and praising in lies in not worshipping and praising in truth come on now. So do better and save you.

All that belongs to life, life must keep and maintain continuously infinitely and indefinitely forever ever without end. Good Life belongs on earth and if you are a part of this good and true life you have to stay on earth. Yes we must clean up earth and this is truly good because earth will become more beautiful than it is now. Good God will show us what to do in goodness and in truth positively infinitely and indefinitely without end. All will be good and clean thus saith the Lord thy God meaning it is so.

Michelle Jean

As I come to the close of this book yet again; I had put this dream from another book in. I think it's befitting. It's October 10, and I am finishing up on this book because I need to finish it.

This is the dream.

Good God it's October 08, 2014 and I dreamt about Prokhorov again. Good God, is this man my true death because somehow I think he is because I keep dreaming about him?

Good God I am not going to hide my thoughts from you because something is not right and you know how I do not like seeing men in black. He was in black and it is crazy not in a bad way but a weird way. We were in his office; place of business in Russia. He was comfortable around me as if we were friends – more than friends but not in a sexual way if that makes any sense. But it makes sense to me. It's weird because he had a prior lunch function. God the food was plenty. He had huge meat shaped in cubes and black women were serving the food. Some of his associates joined him. I was sitting in this chair and this man – white man – older white man say in his fifties or sixties was there. All I saw was him being hit – not with a bullet but with this wire and he fell underneath my chair for dead but he was not dead, he was alive. Hence this dream scares me because it was my chair this man fell under and you could see the blood on the floor from his head. Oh God do I have to fair for my life again?

Is this a new threat to me yet again?

I truly don't know but after that happened, Prokhorov had to go and he told me not to search through his things. He cited depression. Good God he trusted me in the dream because he gave me papers to read but as usual I did not know Russian and he said he's going to have to teach me Russian. But at the end why would he tell me not to search and or look through his things when he had already given me documents to look over and why would he tell me in the dream he was depressed?

Lord I truly don't know what to make of this dream hence I so wanted to go on the defensive in reality and cuss out im BC for insinuating in my dream that I would search through his things. Im nuh noa mi. An dis only a dream but mi nuh search through people's thing so im fi clear off an fine whoa snoop around his financial documents and or business dealings.

I truly do not care if he's depressed. Life is worth living and he should check imself before im reck imself. Disya Jamaican proud of her upbringings and snooping I don't do so Prokhi truly clearoff an guh fine yuself.

No Good God mi vex. Damn wrenk. Do some house cleaning and digging because someone maybe playing you but truly don't look at me. And for me to keep seeing documents with you maybe you truly need to revisit your financial portfolio and do the right thing. You are losing money so truly look into the avenues – areas that are bleeding you financially and let that financial drainage go by selling them.

Family and true loved ones, I truly hate death dreams of this sort because someone is going to die. Maybe someone is going to die or get seriously hurt in one of his factories from a steel pipe or rope. Like I said, it was not a gun that hit this man. It's something made of steel. I don't know if you've seen Cowboys and Aliens but the steel – ribbage of the alien craft is what best describes the object that hits this man. It's not the best description I can give but it's the best I can do. Yes I am lazy, I truly do not want to go back and watch this movie for the exact structure and or configuration of what I saw hit this man. Hence I am going to leave well enough alone.

Prokhorov maybe you need to get your house in order like I said and you need to do it fast because something is not right somewhere in your personal and business life. Hey I am just relaying what I saw and commenting. The rest is truly up to you.

Michelle Jean

Good God, you've shown me many things and many I've included in these books but it's not about me anymore. Like I said, I gave you a mandate of 2015 January 1 to step aside from you because I cannot take the pain; hatred of my people anymore.

I have to have ambition for myself and them including you; hence I tell you to have some ambition of self and do what is best and true for you and your true people. I cannot take the hurt anymore. You see the hurt; you've seen what America has done to its own and other lands. You've seen what other lands have done to their own people in the interest of greed, control and dominance; financial gain – money.

We spy on each other.
We kill each other.
We design nuclear warheads to kill each other
We make atomic bombs to wipe out (destroy and kill) other nations.
We steal from each other.
We lie to each other.
We hate each other and I cannot be party to this anymore.

If this is your true will for man, then I truly have to let you go because you are wrong. And please do not bring up will and the choice and or choices of man – humanity because this could have been prevented long ago.

Like I said, life is worth it and if you cannot see this then something is truly wrong with you and you are not the god for me; truth.

*I've been listening to **Donald Lawrence Encourage Yourself** again. Hence I dedicate Encourage Yourself by Donald Lawrence to you yet again. You have to realize that you are god and you have to do right and just by you. You have to encourage yourself because as humans we are not encouraging you. We lie to you in all that we do and it cannot go on anymore.*

I've told you, if someone does not want you leave them the hell alone to what they want. Yes I know you've done this but you need a little push; encouragement. I truly love you but I cannot let you continue to hurt you when it comes to people that only pretend to want and need you. You are God – Good God so pick yourself up, dust yourself off and live. Truly live for you.

Sometimes look at the trees that are left in Samoa and I am sorry but I have to mention Jamaica. Not out of disrespect but because I still truly love my homeland despite it being forbidden by you. But look at the trees of the mountainside. Look at the sunset of Africa and the animals that still roam free and smile because there is beauty still left on land despite the ills of humanity – humans.

Know the ills of man is not your doing but our own doing hence I tell you to have some ambition and pride in you. You are worth it hence I have to encourage you to do better by you and for you. Your life is worth it. You are life – good life and your are beautiful. So be encouraged because you are great.

You are our true life hence truly listen to the song because all the devil told me about you I know is a lie hence I listen not to them but to you.

You are our help hence I have to lift you up and give you praise. They in humanity may not need you but I need you and I've told you this. Good God you created life out of the waters of life hence you gave us water abundantly not just on earth but in the heavens and in the spiritual realm.

You are the light of the world and universe hence we have light; day and nightlight abundantly.

You are our tree of life hence we have trees abundantly on earth.

You are our air hence we have oxygen on earth.

You are the fruits we eat hence food is abundant on earth.

You are our good all Good God hence I cannot nor will I ever forget you. You need to do you and truly let evil people go. 2015, January 1 is my mandate with you. Yes you've been a good and true friend but I cannot take the hurt and pain anymore. Maybe she, the one that is to save humanity will impact life and get them to change but I cannot. Not because I do not want humanity to change but because we have will; the right to choose good or evil and I too cannot go against a man's will nor can I go against the will of a woman or child. You gave us the right to choose and billions did choose evil over good hence the earth is laden with ills – the sins of man – humanity globally.

I have to step aside for you to do what you need to do for the better good of your people.

I have to step aside and let death do their jobs because female death you know truly don't like me. She's the deadlier of the two deaths. Hence I thread lightly and carefully with her. She's no nonsense and she does not like to be stopped when she's coming. So do what you need to do. You have to because many are crying and dying. Yes many more will die but it's our own choosing not yours. Our sins affect all life hence none truly thought about all life. I have to, hence I plead with you for good and true life. I plead with you to shelter good and true life and let good and true life remain on earth in true peace and harmony.

Good God the killing must stop because the more a person kills, it's the further and longer he or she stays in hell's fire. This is not a fantasy, it's our spirits reality. I've told humanity on numerous occasions the life they live in the living determines where they go in the afterlife; once the spirit sheds the flesh. They (humanity) need to know the truth. We've all sinned Good God but when it comes to environmental sins, sins committed against the earth, I cannot tell them (humans and or humanity) how much time is allotted to them in hell because I truly don't know.

It could be a year but I highly doubt this figure. Earth according to man is billions of years old. So because earth is billions of years old, death can say for each environment sins we commit against earth, we must and will spend 250 billion years burning in hell. Like I said, I truly don't know the time frame hence truly woe be unto man when it comes to environmental sins; sins committed against the earth.

Earth need to replenish herself Good God; but in her replenishing self Good God and Allelujah never ever let any evil hurt her or reside in her ever again for more than forever ever indefinitely. She (Earth) need to rest so let her rest in goodness and in truth forever ever void of all human and spiritual evil, human and spiritual diseases; sins and condemnation.

We need this Good God hence truly help earth in a good and true way.

It's October 12, 2014 and I've been having some weird dreams. This morning I dreamt Sean Paul but I am going to leave Sean Paul alone.

I dreamt this chubby white man. Pleasant man about 36 if not older. He had on a Hawaiian shirt on. I call the shirt Hawaiian because of the yellow. We were talking about the Babylonians and I was getting a bit upset about what he was saying so I had to school (teach) him the truth of the Babylonians starting with Ethiopia. I told him about the white race. Told him not to be racist but the white race like him as in hue brought about death – diseases. The conversation continued and we started to walk and I was liking this guy. He was not well dressed because he had on blue jeans that truly did not fit him. It hung on him in a street way but not too street if that makes sense.

It was weird because in the dream I could see Egypt and these men were in black. I cannot tell you how many men there were but yuk. This dream sick my stomach because you could see the nastiness at the bottom of the soil at the edge. Well I could see it and it was nasty. They the Egyptians laid top soil over the nastiness at the bottom but it was still gross. Yuk. So I don't know if there is going to be a disease outbreak in Egypt and or if they are going to have a mass burial. I truly don't know so if you have an idea or clue let me know. Dear God this was gross because I've never seen anything like.that before in my travels.

Also, the pleasant white man in his yellow multi-coloured shirt told me that Japan and Jamaica is going to be destroyed.

Do not ask me why he told me this but when he said Japan and Jamaica is going to be destroyed I told him humanity is going to be destroyed before 2032.

So if you can make sense of this dream truly let me know. People I know Jamaica is going to be destroyed. Jamaica has been on the chopping block for a while now and I've told you in some of my other books what I saw when it came to this land (Jamaica).

Jamaica was spared when the Tsunami hit Haiti. Trust me they truly don't know what a clock a go strike dem real soon. Twice the island was spared and now that I've stepped aside they are doomed. He the chubby white man just confirmed what I already knew.

Listen, Port Royal is a part of Jamaica's nasty history and Good God and Allelujah gave the people of Jamaica a chance to change their dirty ways but they did not. They kept sinning vile and rude and now that saving grace have and has been revoked. Like I said, in order for the island to be saved they would have to become 99.9% clean like the Lysol in the yellow bottle. And like I said, I have no trust and or faith and or hope in them because I know the wickedness of them.

Port Royal sank in June 1692 because of the wickedness and lawlessness of the buccaneers and pirates that resided on the island. They had no regard for life and morals. Jamaica has not changed because they continue on the road of death without knowing that their evils will one day catch up to them. Yes it will hurt to see the land destroyed but the land and people was deemed unclean by Good God and Allelujah.

In all I've done to relay this message to the people for them to change I've failed, so I have to let it go. It's not that I did not send out books, I did, but like everything else, when you are not mainstream people do not listen to you nor do they give you the time of day.

Hey I tried and failed so I have to let it be; let go.

Do I doubt this man in his saying?

Yes I do because I need to doubt him in a way. I was like Sarah of the bible in the living. Not because of him but because of the length of time it is taking for Jamaica to be destroyed. And yes I did laugh.

<u>I kept remembering the man in black that gave me the noose for Jamaica. He gave me the noose in my hand and the noose disappeared. Maybe the time for death then was not the correct time for Jamaica to be destroyed. Maybe 2015 or 2016 is the time for them to die on a massive scale – be destroyed but who knows. I have to watch time and see and to be honest with you I won't be. I told Good God long ago that when Jamaica is being destroyed, I want to be somewhere warm soaking up the sun because I truly don't want to hear it nor do I want to be found when it happens; Jamaica is destroyed.</u>

Hence I truly hope my doubt of this man does not change the outcome of Jamaica's destruction. Yes there is more that I want and need to say but I will truly leave things here because the wickedness of man unto man has gone on too long. Hence Baby Marley said, "man to man is so unjust" and he told the truth; was correct.

Many things the black race have and has been through at the unjust and unfair treatment of man. These things truly hurt hence I truly hope Good God truly look at the wickedness of the United States Government. Slavery is there Good God; but truly look at the Tuskegee Syphilis Experiment conducted between

1932 to 1972 by the United States Government on your people – the black race. **40 years** *were they subjected to pain and injustice. Now tell me if this is what you Good God call humane; justice?*

Was this a part of your master plan for your people?

How can another human being inject another with their disease and look at themselves in the mirror? Tell me what kind of mercy can anyone have for these demon doctors?

Now let me ask you this. "Is there a place for the hopeless sinner (Bob Marley) – the wicked and evil; condemned in your kingdom?" Yes I know the answer is no but I truly have to ask you because of my pain and tears on this day.

How can you as Good God and Allelujah turn a blind eye to the injustice of one nation? Millions have suffered and lost their lives because of this country but yet you protect them. You treat them as if they are larger than life. You treat them as if you are afraid of them. They no longer house the eye in triangle because they tainted it; tainted life just like my homeland Jamaica.

Now tell me, what about the lives that were lost?

Do you not care? Hence it grieves me for my own. It grieves me to know that you left us behind knowing the inhumane treatment we would face. I know you are not to blame but I have to blame you because I want and need to. How much more do we have to face Good God, How much more? Truly how much more because man to man is truly not just; fair.

We sinned and lost our way. But how can we find our way to you when we truly do not have any hope of survival in this mess if we truly do not have you; can't find you.

I cannot walk with you no more Good God because the tears come and I am truly hurt to know that the one entity that we need is so far from us in all that we do. I need you my people need you and your truth. Please come out of hiding and let us find you. We cannot be the children of the abandoned anymore. We cannot because hell is not our home. We belong with you.

No more begging Good God, I truly can't cry for my own anymore. If you don't want us tell us but do not let us wait in vain for you anymore.

Do not let us succumb to the will of death anymore.

Do not let us continue to think you truly don't care about us.

Do not cause us anymore pain because the pain and heartache we face is truly not needed nor is it worth it; just.

Like I said, I will not forget you but I have to step aside from all of this. I truly need to. You will always be my bestest friend but I have to take another road and journey home. Not in death but in truth, true peace and harmony. I have to be truly clean so if it be thy will, find another someone (her) so she can do all she can to save humanity if this is your will.

Truly thank you for being there for me and protecting me. In all I say and do, I truly hope you find ambition and pride and live like the true king that you were meant to be. Like I've said, if someone truly do not want you, learn to let them go by truly walking away. Yes I know you've done this but truly let go.

You are no one's shit or bitch and no one should class you one. Hence hold your head up because you are my true king and I am truly proud of you and the life you have given me. As humans we've become disrespectful.

We've lost our place with you but yet we are looking to you for help when we value not your laws including you.

Know that you are amazing Good God and I lift my hand to you in joy and say thank you for all you've done for me and humanity no matter the disrespect of man – humanity globally.

Thank you for all you've given me. But more importantly, thank you for life – good life and making me a part of your life and world. I more than love you truthfully and unconditionally. Trust me no universe can contain my true love of you. So chin up, I am with you and on your side of truth and true love all the time.

Hugs and kisses always from your true friend and daughter.

Michelle Jean

OTHER BOOKS BY MICHELLE JEAN

Blackman Redemption – The Fall of Michelle Jean
Blackman Redemption – After the Fall Apology
Blackman Redemption – World Cry – Christine Lewis
Blackman Redemption
Blackman Redemption – The Rise and Fall of Jamaica
Blackman Redemption – The War of Israel
Blackman Redemption – The Way I Speak to God
Blackman Redemption – A Little Talk With Man
Blackman Redemption – The Den of Thieves
Blackman Redemption – The Death of Jamaica
Blackman Redemption – Happy Mother's Day
Blackman Redemption – The Death of Faith
Blackman Redemption – The War of Religion
Blackman Redemption – The Death of Russia
Blackman Redemption – The Truth
Blackman Redemption – Spiritual War
Blackman Redemption – The Youths
Blackman Redemption – Black Man Where Is Your God?

The New Book of Life
The New Book of Life – A Cry For The Children
The New Book of Life – Judgement
The New Book of Life – Love Bound
The New Book of Life – Me
The New Book of Life – Life

Just One of Those Days
Book Two – Just One of Those Days
Just One of Those Days – Book Three The Way I Feel
Just One of Those Days – Book Four

The Days I Am Weak
Crazy Thoughts – My Book of Sin
Broken
Ode to Mr. Dean Fraser

A Little Little Talk
A Little Little Talk – Book Two

Prayers
My Collective
A Little Talk/A Time For Fun and Play
Simple Poems
Behind The Scars
Songs of Praise And Love

Love Bound
Love Bound – Book Two

Dedication Unto My Kids
More Talk
Saving America From A Woman's Perspective
My Collective the Other Side of Me

My Collective the Dark Side of Me
A Blessed Day
Lose To Win
My Doubtful Days – Book One

My Little Talk With God
My Little Talk With God – Book Two

A Different Mood and World – Thinking

My Nagging Day
My Nagging Day – Book Two

Friday September 13, 2013
My True Love
It Would Be You
My Day

A Little Advice – Talk
1313, 2032, 2132 – The End of Man
Tata

MICHELLE'S BOOK BLOG – BOOKS 1 – 19

My Problem Day
A Better Way
Stay – Adultery and the Weight of Sin – Cleanliness Message

Let's Talk
Lonely Days – Foundation
A Little Talk With Jamaica – As Long As I Live
Instructions For Death